**the information store**

☎ 01603 773114
email: tis@ccn.ac.uk

21 DAY LOAN ITEM

Please return <u>on or before</u> the last date stamped above

A fine will be charged for overdue items

 CITY COLLEGE NORWICH

of related interest

Asperger's Syndrome
A Guide for Parents and Professionals
Tony Attwood
Foreword by Lorna Wing
ISBN 1 85302 577 1

Pretending to be Normal
Living with Asperger's Syndrome
Liane Holliday Willey
Foreword by Tony Attwood
ISBN 1 85302 749 9

Bright Splinters of the Mind
A Personal Story of Research with Autistic Savants
Beate Hermelin
Foreword by Sir Michael Rutter
ISBN 1 85302 932 7

Hitchhiking Through Asperger Syndrome
Lise Pyles
Foreword by Tony Attwood
ISBN 1 85302 937 8

Asperger Syndrome, The Universe and Everything
Kenneth Hall
Forewords by Kenn P. Kerr and Gill Rowley
ISBN 1 85302 930 0

A Different Kind of Boy

A Father's Memoir on Raising a Gifted Child with Autism

Daniel Mont

Jessica Kingsley Publishers
London and Philadelphia

The right of Daniel Mont to be identified as the author of this work has been asserted by him in accordance with the Copyright, Designs and Patents Act 1988.

First published in the United Kingdom in 2002
by Jessica Kingsley Publishers Ltd
116 Pentonville Road
London N1 9JB, England
and
325 Chestnut Street
Philadelphia, PA 19106, USA

www.jkp.com

Copyright © Daniel Mont 2002

Library of Congress Cataloging in Publication Data
A CIP catalog record for this book is available from the Library of Congress

British Library Cataloguing in Publication Data
A CIP catalogue record for this book is available from the British Library

ISBN 1 84310 715 5

Printed and Bound in Great Britain by
Athenaeum Press, Gateshead, Tyne and Wear

Contents

*To my mom and dad, my first and best
teachers on being a parent,
and Nanette, Alex, and Simon*

Acknowledgements

In sitting down to write these acknowledgements, I've been reminded how blessed I am with friends and family. Many people read parts of this book in its various incarnations, but I am especially grateful to Evi Strauss and Steve Smith who offered extensive editorial suggestions on multiple versions, as well as emotional support. Theresa Hammond was another early, continued, and enthusiastic source of encouragement. Ted Kamp led me to his brother David who in turn led me to Todd Shuster, all of whom provided me with valued assistance shaping the book. I was especially grateful for David's help, whom I only remembered from my childhood as Ted's little brother who made underground comic books.

The people who read sections of this book (or who had sections read to them over the phone) or who encouraged me in my efforts to write and then publish it include my sister and her family, Debbie, Sam, Rebecca, and Jessica Kirzner, and also Lori Boyd, Mel Cathey, Carol Frost, Merle Goodman, Phil Greene, Polly Hodges, Brian Karem, Susan Labovich, Fred Marshall, Alan Mathios, Leah Mazade, Jay Noell, and Marcia Regenstein.

Three of Alex's teachers, Eileen Bagley, Joanne Stocklin, and Amy Giblin were kind enough to get together for dinner one night and discuss what it was like to have Alex in their classes.

My employers at the National Academy of Social Insurance – in particular Pam Larson and Virginia Reno – were exceptionally gracious in allowing me to arrange my work schedule in a fashion that permitted me to have significant blocks of time to work on this project.

Finally, my deepest and most heartfelt thanks goes to my wife Nanette and to our sons Alex and Simon. Needless to say without them this book would have been impossible. They were my fact checkers and my inspiration. They allowed me to tell our story. But most importantly, they are the loves of my life.

1

A Fair-Haired Boy

CԸ

The elementary school gym quickly fills with long lines of children as they file through the doorway and take their seats on the floor. They giggle and squirm and poke each other. One little boy proudly displays a rubber alien to one of his friends. Soon the room reverberates with the tinny sound of hundreds of high-pitched conversations, as the teachers try to straighten the rows of children.

The principal, a middle-aged woman with short, light-colored hair, steps up to a microphone at the front of the room. Immediately, teachers and teachers' pets raise their index fingers to their lips.

"Shhhhh!"

The room quiets down. As the principal gets ready to speak, a blast of feedback from the microphone elicits a scattering of chuckles.

"Welcome, boys and girls," the principal says in the singsong voice some adults use when speaking to children. "Now settle down and show our guests your best Candlewood behavior."

The guests are parents who are sitting in metal chairs lined around the periphery of the room. This is the end of the year assembly – time for the last batch of "Soaring Eagle Awards."

One by one or in groups, children are called to the front of the room to be honored for their academic excellence or participation in band, dance, or the soccer club. They walk proudly to the microphone, which is set up under a basketball hoop, and receive their awards from the teachers in charge of the various activities. Then, they scurry back to their seats to show them to their friends.

The math team coaches are introduced. A tall, lanky and balding teacher with glasses grabs a stack of certificates. He's wearing a brightly colored tie, and when he talks he makes large, sweeping gestures.

"First of all," he says, "I think we should have a round of applause for all the fourth and fifth grade boys and girls who took part in this year's National Math Olympiad – a very challenging math competition that takes place all across America." After a polite round of clapping subsides, he calls out the children's names and hands out the certificates. A few children are singled out for scoring high enough to earn special patches.

"And now, I'd like to give out a special award."

Eyes turn towards a little nine-year-old boy sitting on his teacher's lap. He leans forward like a sprinter, ready to leap to the front of the room. He has blond hair and a round face. His blue-gray eyes are wide open behind bent and dirty spectacles. His shoes are untied and his T-shirt, which displays the solar system and a chart containing a host of numeric data on the planets, is barely halfway tucked into his jeans. He's short, and he's ready.

"For the first time in school history we had a student get a perfect score on the National Math Olympiad, one of a very few students in the whole country to do so. Alex Mont, will you step up here please?"

The fair-haired boy runs to the front of the room as the audience erupts into cheers. He claps his hands to his ears and grabs the award, never making eye contact with anyone. He is obviously excited but he struggles to hide a smile. Hesitatingly, he starts off back to his seat. His teacher starts to wipe her eyes as the clapping continues.

The little boy looks down at the floor, uncomfortable with the attention. The room is filled with children who like and respect him, but he has no real friends. He can barely name anyone in his class – even children he has been with for three years. He has trouble with the simplest things – recognizing people, pretending, and knowing when people are happy or angry or sad. He can't tell the good guys from the bad guys in movies. He is only beginning to talk on the phone. Much of his life has been filled with anxiety. He's out of step with the world, which to him is mostly a whirlwind that must be actively decoded and put into order.

And yet, 85,000 students participated in the National Math Olympiad and he was one of only seven fourth graders in the nation to ace the test. In the fifth grade, he finished second in the country out of 9000 of the nation's top students who were invited to take part in a talent search sponsored by the Johns Hopkins University. He's a boy who has reveled and delighted in math since he was a toddler – who was using logarithms in kindergarten, finding mistakes in books on probability when he was six years old, and solving complex problems while shopping in the grocery store as he giggled into his hands and rolled on the floor.

That boy is my son, Alex. Alex is autistic. Alex is also loving, brilliant and resilient. He has taught me a great deal about life, about what it means to connect with other people and about how one builds a life that suits oneself. Through raising Alex I've learned about a lot of things – how the mind works, how special education should work, the generosity of children, and – oh, yes, math. Lots about math.

★★★★★

Upon hearing the term "autistic" most people conjure up visions of people who are totally shut off from the world. People with no language, who rock incessantly or maybe bang their heads against the wall. People who are not capable of functioning in the world at large.

Some autistic people are like that. But autism actually encompasses a broad range of abilities. Some autistic people are college professors or computer programmers. Some are married. All of them, though, have trouble dealing with the world of the NT, that is, the neurologically typical. Temple Grandin, an autistic woman who has written several books on the subject, has described being autistic as being "an anthro-pologist on Mars."* She feels her brain is wired differently from the NTs, and the way they communicate with each other and behave is at some deep level a mystery to her. She copes, though, by observing them as an anthropologist would. She uncovers the rituals and behav-iors of typical people and then learns to incorporate those behaviors in many different "scripts" that she uses in different situations. One autistic person, writing to an internet chat group, said he had ascertained through careful observation that in conversations with NTs eye contact was important at the beginning of a speech and at the end, but seemed optional during the course of the speech. There's a handy tidbit of information guaranteed to help you glide through life. Now let's decode irony. Or sarcasm. Or, as my child had great difficulty with – the difference between lying and pretending. Explain that one in rock solid language to a six-year-old. I guarantee you it is harder than you first think.

I'm getting ahead of myself here, however. I am not an expert on autism. I am, though, an expert on Alex. At least as much as any NT could be.

* Sacks, O. (1996) *An Anthropologist on Mars*. New York: Vintage Books.

2

"You're a Father Now, Damn it!"

○ʒ

I'll never forget the day we brought Alex home from the hospital. He was our first child and so naturally we were excited, nervous, and just a tad shy of being overwhelmed. I could not believe the people at the hospital were allowing us to bring him home – entrusting this new life to us. I was twenty-six and suddenly felt very young and too inexperienced for such an important task.

It was October of 1987, and the air had suddenly turned crisp. I drove down to the hospital, the brand new car seat strapped snugly into the back seat of our car, and pulled up to the front entryway. Nanette, Alex, and a nurse were already waiting for me. The nurse checked that I had put in our new infant seat properly, and wished us luck. Bursting with excitement, we gently buckled him in and headed back to the apartment – the three of us – a family. When we got home we removed the little Ernie doll that had been saving his place in the crib and set him down sleeping. We looked at each other. Now what? Weren't we supposed to be doing something? What key parenting activity should we engage in? These were typical first parent thoughts. Unfortunately, Alex's birth was not exactly typical.

Nanette's labor did not go as planned. Late the night before she had noticed some clear liquid leaking down her leg.

"Did your water break?"

"I don't think so."

"What do you mean, you don't think so?"

"Well, our Lamaze instructor said if you can stop the flow by trying to hold it in then it isn't amniotic fluid, it's just urine."

"Does it smell like urine?"

"No...I don't think so."

"Well, what should we do?"

"I have a doctor's appointment tomorrow first thing in the morning. I don't want to rush to the hospital and find out my water isn't broken. I mean, it's supposed to gush out, right? Let me go back to sleep and I'll find out tomorrow."

The next morning we drove down to the doctor's office. Nanette's doctor was a jovial man in his late fifties who looked like he played football in his youth. His son was a star athlete at the university and that night was the biggest game of the season.

"Now don't tell me you're in labor," he chuckled. "I told you that you can't give birth tonight."

"Well, actually," said Nanette, "I'm not sure, but I think my water may have broken."

Concern flashed across his face. "Not sure? Get undressed." Nanette started to explain about what the Lamaze instructor said, but before she could say much he told us that her water had broken. He told us to get to the hospital immediately. He was going to induce labor.

Nanette dilated slowly. After a few hours it was clear that the doctor was not going to make his son's game and he began getting surly. During that time her labor pains were mostly in her legs. The nurses thought this was a sign that the baby was not coming out in the proper position, but the doctor ignored those concerns. Nurses whispered in the hallway outside the hospital room door, as Nanette screamed in agony. I could feel panic bubbling up to the surface.

"Excuse me, but what are you talking about?"

"We think if your wife doesn't dilate further very soon she's going to need an emergency C-section."

"Just do it," I thought. I only wanted a healthy baby and a healthy mom. I went back inside to be with Nanette, trying to hide my concern.

They soon measured her again. She had dilated further and she was entering the last phases of labor – just in time to avoid the C-section. They rushed her down the hall. Sweat poured from her face, which was red from the labor pains. She looked relieved though. The baby was finally on its way.

"Okay, now push." The doctor spoke firmly. The baby wasn't coming. He realized that Alex was facing sideways and would not come out. He reached for his forceps and yanked Alex out quickly. Nanette screamed. Although she had had an episiotomy, she ripped further. The labor nurse stared with the focus of a laser beam into Nanette's eyes and said, "Don't move!" Their eyes locked together as the doctor sutured an unanesthetized Nanette.

I felt about as useful as an icemaker on the Titanic.

Meanwhile Alex was experiencing his first few minutes in the world. Wrinkled, slimy, and crying he was being wrapped in a blanket. Proud dad feelings started welling up inside me. He was beautiful.

Something was wrong, though. His left arm hung limply by his side.

"What's wrong with his arm? Will he be able to move it?"

"We don't know."

People are usually not that straight with you. I was expecting an answer more along the lines of "We can't say for sure but he'll probably be just fine". The honesty was a bit jarring. In the future, there would be times I would have appreciated that much honesty.

The rest of the day is a bit of a blur. Nanette started recuperating and mercifully seemed to have little recollection of exactly how much pain she had been in. She actually said, "That wasn't as bad as I'd expected."

"Where were *you*?" I asked. Maybe not the most sensitive of things to say. She was feeling better, though; we had called our immediate family, and Alex was resting with what we hoped was just a broken arm.

We had planned on calling a lot more people, but decided against it.

"If I have to explain about his arm one more time..." Nanette pulled the pale blue hospital gown over her shoulders. She was sitting up on a stretcher in the recovery room.

"I know, it takes the fun out of calling. I don't feel like reassuring people or being reassured right now. Why don't we just wait until we have more news."

"I knew something was going to go wrong."

Throughout the pregnancy, in the back of our minds, we had worried about potential problems. One of Nanette's nephews is mentally retarded and my younger sister had serious emotional problems throughout her childhood. Both of them required monumental efforts. Both of them caused considerable strain. We had intimate experience with families with children with special needs, and we did not feel invulnerable.

That night, after I had gone home and was already asleep, I was awakened by a phone call. It was Nanette, and she was crying. I snapped to alertness. Something was wrong with Alex. My beautiful little baby boy.

"You're a father now, damn it," I thought, "you've got to be in control. You've got to be strong for Alex and Nanette."

I threw some clothes on and rushed down to the hospital. The streets were deserted. The drive seemed eerily interminable. I parked the car in the deck and ran to Nanette's room. She was sitting up in bed, pale, her hands clutching some wadded tissues. At the sight of me she burst into tears.

"What's wrong, sweetie?"

I sat next to her, and she told me. Alex's arm had swelled during the night and the doctors were afraid that maybe he had an infection. Several hours had elapsed between the time Nanette's water had broken and when she got to the hospital and so for a while Alex may have been in a non-sterile environment. They had taken Alex to neonatal intensive care and started giving him antibiotics intravenously as a precaution. If he had an infection they did not want it to reach the brain. If the doctors had been too late in prescribing the antibiotics and the infection did reach the brain, the consequences could be very severe.

"This can't be happening," I thought. "He's going to be OK."

I felt sick, but I was resolved not to show Nanette the extent to which I was worried.

"Don't think the worst. It'll be OK."

We walked down the hall, arm in arm, to look at him through the neonatal nursery window. Nanette was hobbling from childbirth pains. Alex's arm was strapped to a small Styrofoam board; he had an IV going into it.

He looked like a giant in there with all the prematurely born babies. Seeing the other children helped keep things in focus, actually. As long as he received the antibiotics in time, he would be fine. Maybe he didn't even have an infection.

"I'm such an idiot. I didn't even know my own water broke."

"You're not an idiot. You never had a baby before. And the Lamaze instructor said…"

"And that damned game. He was so damned annoyed that he was missing it!"

I approach conflict slowly, and I didn't want to talk about the doctor; I wanted to talk about the baby.

"There's no use in blaming anyone right now…"

"What do you mean! He was annoyed as hell!"

"I know. I know. But I can't think about that now…we don't even know for sure that there's anything serious."

I went home again that night, threw the keys on the table, and sat down in front of the television. I couldn't concentrate so I walked down the hall and lay down on the mattress that was our bed, staring at the ceiling. From time to time, a car would drive through the parking lot and briefly shine its headlights through the bedroom window.

An infection in the brain? I couldn't think of a worse nightmare.

In the early hours of the morning, I lay staring out the window. Meanwhile, back in the hospital, our pediatrician came to see Nanette. He was a thin man with a thin, reddish beard and a Dutch accent. We had chosen him on the recommendation of several people.

"Nanette?" His manner was soft but direct.

"Yes?"

"I have some good news for you."

"Really?"

"Yes. You have a healthy baby boy, who may never move his right arm."

Nanette called me on the phone.

"A healthy baby boy who may never move his arm? That's what he said to you?" I was poised to be pissed.

"Yes, but it was the perfect thing to say."

"Why?"

"I don't know. It just put everything in perspective. I'm so relieved. He's going to be OK. There was no infection. They said he has brachial plexus palsy. That son of a bitch obstetrician yanked him out so hard he pulled the nerve in his shoulder."

"He had to get him out. It was an emergency."

"Come on. The nurses were trying to tell him the baby wasn't coming out correctly hours before. They knew there were problems. He wouldn't listen."

"You're right. You're right. But he said there's no infection, right? It's just his arm."

"No. There's no infection."

Later, we discovered that the swelling was only the result of a broken bone. The doctors could not make the diagnosis earlier because newborns' bones are made totally of cartilage. That makes it impossible to tell by using an X-ray if they are broken until the bones begin to heal.

In the end, the paralysis of Alex's arm was short-lived. Luckily, with the help of a daily range of motion exercises, all the movement came back within the next six months.

Later, however, we learned that some evidence suggests that autism is correlated with heavy doses of antibiotics in infants.

Is that the case with Alex? We'll never know. The causes of autism are complex and not well understood. Some genetic proclivity seems to exist. For example, if parents have one autistic child, there is a 2 per cent chance that any additional children they have will also be autistic, a much higher rate than in the general population. Some researchers believe that different environmental stimuli – for example vaccines or antibiotics – can trigger that proclivity, allowing the autism to manifest itself. These findings are not rock solid, by any means, but you would think that they would gnaw away at our insides. They don't. The cause of Alex's autism is not that important to us. As a matter of fact, I feel uncomfortable even writing the phrase "Alex's autism." You cannot separate autism from Alex. It is not like an appendage. It is fundamentally a part of who he is. In that regard, it's part of what we love about him. To take away Alex's autism would be to change his essence. Of course, that's not how we felt when we originally got the diagnosis of autism – and it took some autistic adults to help us come to that understanding. But, let's get back to the story. Alex's arm was OK. He was a healthy baby. He was home. He was sleeping in the crib, and we felt like we needed to be doing some sort of parenting. Silly us. We should have been taking a nap.

3

The Wild Goose Chase

ℭℨ

Nanette and I met in graduate school in Madison, Wisconsin, late in the summer of 1984. She was entering the PhD program in economics after taking two years off after college, and I was a second year student in the same program who had plunged ahead immediately upon graduation. We both were assigned to be teaching assistants for the same introductory economics course.

Madison is a clean, beautiful, university town surrounded by four lakes and ribboned with bike paths. Every Saturday morning in warm weather a vibrant farmer's market surrounds the State Capitol. I loved walking around sampling the freshly baked breads and muffins, and sorting through the booths crammed with crisp, colorful vegetables, Wisconsin cheese and locally made crafts. I'd meet friends and we'd sit on the lawn having breakfast. It was my favorite part of the city.

In the cold, blustery months, the lakes froze over and the wind whipped through my body like a chainsaw. Oddly enough, the streets didn't become deserted. On my way up to school, as I ducked from one building to the next to shield myself from the cold, I was passed by cross-country skiers on their way to work and cyclists with ski masks and snow tires. Eventually, I learned to embrace the winter and got my own pair of skis. If you don't embrace the winter in Wisconsin, it can suffocate you.

Being economics doctoral candidates, Nanette and I felt suffocated enough. The workload was heavy and very technical, and the pressure of qualifying exams constantly loomed in the distance. The cold, dark months of winter were filled with mathematical proofs, never-ending problem sets, and a series of workshops where graduate students' ideas for dissertations were picked apart, probed, and only occasionally praised.

Nanette struck me as an energetic, upbeat person with a marvelous sense of humor and an infectious laugh. She had long dark hair, glasses, and an earthy look about her. Always dressed comfortably in jeans, her body fit from a summer at an Outward Bound camp, she seemed ready to try anything.

Our first date did not really start off as a date. Winter was approaching and I knew that soon we'd all be hunkering down. In late fall, huge flocks of Canadian Geese collect at Horicon Marsh, not that far from Madison, and thousands and thousands of honking birds fill the skies before heading south for the winter. I thought it would be cool to organize a trip to ride out to Horicon, see the geese, and escape from microeconomic theory and econometrics for a day. I rounded up a group of people, including Nanette.

The day of our excursion came and one by one everyone called to cancel. Everyone except Nanette…you see, she was the one with a car. I suppose that in the final analysis, my classmates did not find geese compelling. Neither did Nanette. She also wanted to cancel but felt obligated to come because she was driving.

Nanette pulled up in front of my house in her white Toyota Celica and beeped the horn. I ran out and hopped in the front seat.

"So who do we pick up next?" She asked.

"Well, everybody else called and said they couldn't make it."

"Everybody?"

"Yeah."

"Really."

I have to admit that I was secretly pleased.

We decided to go. We hit the road and quickly got lost. We were out in the middle of nowhere amidst cornfields and cows and couldn't even find a place to eat. The day could easily have been a disaster but instead it was filled with laughter and chemistry. After finally finding the Wild Goose Parkway – the irony of the name did not escape us – we arrived at Horicon Marsh and saw one pathetically small flock of geese. In the end, though, the day was quite a success.

I was at the end of a long-distance relationship with my college sweetheart at the time so Nanette and I actually didn't start seeing each other until February, after that relationship had ended. But Nanette stuck in my mind continually from that day. By August we were engaged and by the following June we were married.

After we were married, it wasn't long before we began thinking about starting a family. We both had a strong urge to have children. I've always loved kids. While I was in graduate school I volunteered with and eventually was the coordinator for the Men's Childcare Collective. We were a group of men that provided free childcare for various lefty concerns – concerts, political activities, the battered women's shelter, and of course a long list of support groups.

But now, I had my own child, which was a totally different thing.

4

A Different Sort of Boy

CB

Alex was our first child. I had never really known another infant. All my time doing childcare for toddlers and little boys and girls seemed irrelevant. And Alex was mine. Every movement and sigh was a major event.

Like typical young parents we had a stack of books outlining what your baby was supposed to be doing on a month by month basis. At first I read them religiously but after a few months I stopped looking at them. Alex seemed basically on track, but I feared getting neurotic about his being a few weeks late for one milestone or absurdly proud because he was a few weeks early on something else. I figured we were all better off if I just relaxed and enjoyed him. Besides, he was healthy, his arm had made remarkable progress, and he seemed to be a very content little guy.

It wasn't long, though, before the first glimmers of concern materialized. Looking back we are amazed we didn't start searching out expert help at an even earlier age.

At first, we thought he had hearing problems. He often was non-responsive, but not consistently so.

"He's not deaf. He responds to his name," Nanette said, "But maybe he's a little hard of hearing."

"Let me sneak up behind him."

Alex would be sitting in his high chair, munching on an animal cracker or mushed bananas, and I'd creep up behind him.

"Alex!"

Sometimes he turned around and sometimes he didn't.

One day, early in spring Nanette had taken Alex down to the park to hook up with a friend of hers who also had a little boy, slightly older than Alex. The long, cold Madison winter had just ended. The lakes were no longer frozen over, and the boys didn't need to be bundled up. When a plane flew overhead, Nanette noticed that her friend's child jerked his head back to look. Alex, on the other hand, was oblivious. She made it a point after that to observe other kids when a plane went by or when a truck or bus came down a quiet street. They always turned their heads to the sound. Alex didn't. He just kept batting the toys attached to his stroller or chewing on a cracker. We were unnerved.

Eventually we convinced ourselves that hearing wasn't the problem. Hearing tests later confirmed our conclusions. We chalked up his occasional non-response to his exceptional ability to focus on whatever he was doing. He would stare at things – often spinning things – with an uncanny concentration.

Alex differed from other kids in other ways, too. He never cooed or babbled. He never said nonsense words or played by making sounds. I got down on the floor with him or sat him on my lap.

"Hi, Alex. Are you a big boy?"

He stared back with big steel-blue eyes, silent. Even when he enjoyed an activity he expressed no feelings. He loved to swing, for example. We had one of those crank-up swings. He'd go back and forth interminably, sitting motionless, nestled in a soft, brightly colored blanket, maybe with a stuffed animal by his side that he completely ignored. His smooth, delicate face would be as motionless as a china doll, as he swung on and on, his eyes fixed dead straight ahead.

If we stopped the swing he would cry out, but he never, ever smiled or laughed. We saw other children laugh or wave their pudgy little arms, but not Alex. We'd see other kids chortle their way through endless games of peek-a-boo, their whole beings lighting up at never-ending repetitions of their parents poking their faces out from behind a towel. Alex just watched.

And the boy was intense. Even before he was a year old he could maintain his attention on something for over an hour. Most children bop from activity to activity or are easily distracted by a new toy or funny sound. By the time he was a toddler, though, he would focus intensely and exclusively on one activity for a few hours in a row. When he was engaged, he was in a zone.

Staring at the tape player enthralled him, for example. Eventually, it became apparent that the music was irrelevant. What he enjoyed was watching the tape spin and the counter cycle through the numbers. In front of the tape deck, Alex would smile. He did laugh, but at unusual things. And as odd as watching the tape counter was, at least it brought us some relief from the non-stop demands of caring for a baby. We could actually talk with friends on those rare occasions when we got together with someone for dinner.

The love of spinning objects, showing few emotions, and not babbling, are telltale signs of autism, but we didn't know it at the time. Alex would crawl all over the apartment looking for things that he thought he might be able to spin. He'd pick up a bowl, a ball, the lid of a pot – anything with a rounded surface – and carry it, crawling, to the kitchen. That was the only room in our apartment that wasn't carpeted. He'd have some object in his hand or tucked under his arm and he'd awkwardly make his way to the kitchen with a look of determination on his face. Repeatedly (and I mean *repeatedly*) he would try to throw, roll, or spin it. If he were successful in creating the desired spin his face would come alive.

"See, Nanette, he gets excited about things. He loves making those lids spin."

"Yeah, he never gets tired of that."

"It's like he's conducting experiments. He's a little physicist."

One day, trying to capitalize on his love of spinning things I sat down on the floor with him and took out a plastic cup. With a quick movement, I put a hard backspin on the cup. Alex erupted in glee. Robin Williams doesn't get laughs like this playing to a soused audience.

"Nanette, come look at this. He's hysterical! He's actually laughing."

"Try it with a ball."

"Do you think he thinks it's so funny because he doesn't expect the ball to reverse directions like that?"

"He's laughing like a maniac! Does he know enough to know what to expect?"

Needless to say, I became the king of kitchen floor backspin. We thought it was cute. We loved to see him laugh. We were amazed at his staying power. We didn't know it was symptomatic of autism.

At first, many of Alex's characteristics seemed as if they were signs of his being precocious. His fixation on books for instance. We first read Alex a book when he was four months old. He couldn't even sit up yet. We have a picture of this little blob of a boy nestled in my lap, leaning on my chest with me holding a book in front of him. He'd want me to read this book to him over and over again. The entire time his attention would be focussed on the page, completely rapt. When I tried to stop he would complain. Unbelievably, he learned to turn the pages of his favorite books at the appropriate time when he was just shy of a year. I should say he tried to turn the pages. He didn't have the fine motor coordination to do so yet.

"He can't possibly remember the end of each page, Nanette."

"I know. Maybe he can tell by the cadence of our voice. Or maybe we pause a little bit, but he is definitely trying to turn the page. Watch. And he does it at the right time."

"Well, we've read him these books a thousand times."

I was finishing my dissertation and Nanette was working full-time. That left me as the primary caretaker most of the day and much of that day was spent reading. I loved reading to Alex. I loved the warmth of his little body close to mine, the soft wisps of hair that brushed across my chin as he sat, completely motionless in my lap, facing forward as I held the book open in front of us.

His love of reading thrilled me. I kept thinking how bright he must be. But after a while the time we spent reading was getting to be too much. I wanted to play with blocks, too. And to be perfectly honest, I wanted some moments to myself. Alex took short and infrequent naps.

His constant need for attention – and the complete attention that our reading together entailed – was beginning to string me out. Alex wanted to be read to for hours. Hours and hours, several times a day. His favorite author was Dr Seuss, but he loved anything with a regular rhyme.

Alex was eleven months old. It got to the point where Nanette and I competed to see who could recite the most Dr Seuss books from cover to cover. Later we learned that this was a common experience among parents of high-functioning children with autism.

I didn't think Alex's extreme love of books was a sign of any developmental problem, but my brain was starting to get freeze-dried by hours of reading those interminable rhymes. My life was being taken over by the incessant rhythm of those books.

"Please, Alex let us sit and play,

I do not want to read today,

I do not, do not want to read,

I beg, implore, beseech and plead!"

It sounds funny in retrospect, but the incessant rhythm was starting to feel like Chinese water torture. Sitting still for that many hours made me want to crawl out of my skin. My only alternatives, though, were to place him in his swing or set him in front of the tape deck. I felt guilty, though. Shouldn't I be stimulating this child? What was I doing wrong that made him indifferent to playing with toys? Why couldn't he amuse himself for ten minutes? Was I spoiling him? Or maybe, was I looking at him and at myself a little too closely, like a typically overeducated baby boomer.

Occasionally I tried letting him cry by himself, alone on a blanket, hoping he would resign himself to the fact that he needed to play by himself from time to time, but he never calmed down. And except for the backspin game, he wouldn't even play with toys with *me*. Why would he start doing it by himself? I was relegated to day after day of diapers and Dr Seuss.

One day I tried to get some professional help from a child psychologist on a National Public Radio call-in show. I was home alone with my kid. I was desperate.

"Hello. I have a problem that may not sound like much of a problem. You see, my child, who is eleven months old, loves to read all the time."

"Well, you're right. That sounds like a problem most parents would love to have."

"I know. I'm thrilled that he loves to read. The problem is he wants to read non-stop for hours and hours each day. Mostly Dr Seuss. I'm going out of my mind and I'm worried that my son will start picking up these bad vibes. I don't want to unintentionally send him the message that Daddy doesn't like to read but I am really, really starting to lose it."

"Well," she says after a little laugh, "you could try keeping the books out of sight and then only pull them out during special reading times."

"I tried that. At first I put them in the shelves with the adult books, but he found them. He'd crawl over to the bookcase and pull out a Dr Seuss book and push it in front of him as he headed my way. So then, I hid them completely. The poor little guy was crawling over the whole house looking for them, very upset. I felt ridiculous."

She tried to give me more advice but she was very light-hearted about it. I couldn't blame her. In a way, it sounded like I was bragging, but I wasn't.

A few calls after me a woman phoned in. "You shouldn't have laughed at that father who called in earlier," she said. "I have a child remarkably like his and it is a big problem. It can drive you nuts."

I wish I knew that woman's name. I'd love to get in touch with her. Judging from my experiences with other parents, I'd bet her child is autistic.

5

Daycare

CB

It quickly became apparent that any notion I had of finishing my dissertation while being home with Alex was ludicrous. Even if he had been a typical child it would probably have been impossible. I resigned myself to an extra year of graduate school, but we had to come up with a more workable childcare arrangement.

Nanette was doing statistical work for an agency monitoring the Medicaid program in Wisconsin and bringing in the only real paycheck. I was teaching a night course on labor economics at the University of Wisconsin – Milwaukee, which involved commuting over an hour in each direction. Free time was scarce, and working on a dissertation requires a schedule with fairly reliable blocks of time to get down to work. Nanette was eager to stay home with Alex, and I desperately wanted to finish my dissertation, which was hanging like a huge stone around my neck.

The solution, we thought, was daycare. Nanette and I both felt uncomfortable with full-time daycare, and could not afford it. Besides, Alex, who was still shy of a year, did not seem to care for other children. Even adults – aside from the two of us – had a hard time comforting him. We didn't expect him to love daycare, but I needed the time. And maybe, we thought, this would get him used to other children – or at least interested in other things.

We visited a bunch of providers. We started with family providers, thinking that Alex would get a little more attention there.

"Well, that was depressing," I said.

"I can't believe it. It looks like they all just sit in front of the TV all day."

"At least it was clean. That last place didn't even look baby-proof."

"I don't know, Dan, we're probably going to have to look at daycare centers, too. But he's so little."

We found a place with large rooms and lots of light, airy space. The children there seemed happy and engaged, and the infant room, where Alex would be, was clean, well-stocked, and staffed by a couple of charming young women.

"I think this is the place, Dan."

"You're right."

We met with the director, signed Alex up, and paid for the first month. He'd only be attending part-time. It wasn't what we had envisioned, but we felt comfortable.

Alex's first morning at daycare arrived. We packed his diaper bag and fed him Gerber's rice cereal with mushed pears mixed in. Nanette kissed him and headed off for work. I loaded him in the car with all his stuff, and drove to the daycare building. It was on a major road across from a lake on one side and the Dairy Expo on the other.

"Good-bye, big guy."

I gave him a hug, set him down on the floor next to a pile of toys and a two-foot-high plastic slide, kissed him on the forehead, and waved good-bye. As I left the room I heard him begin to scream. "That's typical," I thought. "It's just separation anxiety. He'll get used to it." Still, I had a lump in my throat as I glanced back over my shoulder through the large glass windows of the infant room. I paused for a moment outside and brushed off my concern. Then I headed back to my car. "He'll be fine," I thought. "As soon as I'm out of sight, I'll be out of mind."

The idea of doing schoolwork all day was almost indulgent. I headed up to my office and tried to get as much done as possible. I was nearing the end of my dissertation, "Two-Earner Family Migration: A Search Theoretic and Empirical Analysis".

When I returned to pick up Alex, I expected to find him happy. He wasn't.

"Has he been crying all day?"

"No," said the daycare worker. "He cried quite a bit but he also hung out on the playmat. Actually, he slept most of the day."

"Slept? He never takes long naps."

"Well, this is his first day. It's all new to him. He'll get used to it."

That's right, I thought. Eventually he would acclimate himself. As the weeks went by, though, that never happened. I left him screaming in the morning and returned to find him teary-eyed. This went on for months. He wanted no part of the other children, slept most of the morning, and wasn't even that receptive to being cuddled by his caregivers.

"I don't think he's happy there, Nanette."

Nanette went to talk to the teachers. They tried to be reassuring but the picture they painted of Alex's day did not put Nanette at ease. Luckily, we thought, this was only a temporary situation.

I tried to get a lot of work done, so I could justify picking him up early, but I knew the best thing I could do for him was to finish my dissertation as fast as possible. Nanette wanted nothing more than to be at home with him. That meant I had to start earning a real salary, and not just be a lecturer at night school.

"It's just a few more months, Nanno. Then you'll be a full-time mom. Lots of children are in daycare."

"You know as well as I do that Alex never sleeps that much. So why is he sleeping most of the time at daycare? It's because he is unhappy."

"I'm almost finished and then this will be over."

Eventually my dissertation progressed to the point where I was merely tying up loose ends. A completion date seemed inevitable instead of unattainable. We pulled Alex out of daycare and started saying good-bye to Madison.

The future that summer seemed bright. Alex was closing in on his second birthday. We would take him to the farmer's market, buy breakfast or lunch and hang out on the lawn, maybe listening to street per-formers. Usually, we'd run into friends who would "ooh" and "ahh" over how big Alex was getting. He was healthy and strong, the last vestiges of his paralysis long gone, and I was finally about to leave my student days.

I was hired as an assistant professor at Cornell University in Ithaca, New York, with the job starting at the end of the summer. We packed our bags, put Alex in the back seat of the Toyota, and headed out east. I was delighted to be launching my career, and we both were delighted that Nanette would be home with Alex. She wanted very much to be a full-time stay-at-home mom, and, well, Alex seemed to need special attention.

6

An Addition to the Family

❧

When we moved to Ithaca in the summer of 1989, Nanette was in the third trimester of her second pregnancy. We bought a house on the outskirts of town that sat on over an acre of land, in an area called Ellis Hollow. It was a small, charming house with a wood stove, three bedrooms, wooden floors, and a family room. The front bay window looked out across a meadow with a hill in the background. Our backyard bordered a wooded area with large old trees. We had a fenced-in patch of blueberry bushes and our lawn was dotted with tiny wild strawberries. A family of foxes lived in the meadow. Just down the road was a small creek.

We set up Alex's room and what would eventually be Simon's nursery. Nanette had made a quilt with a hot-air balloon on it that we hung across from Alex's bed. We scurried around trying to get everything ready for "number two" as I prepared my notes for the course I was teaching that fall. My first publication had recently come out in the *Journal of Population Economics*. It was a time of expectancy.

One of the things we were expecting was a reaction from Alex when we brought the new baby home. Alex would be nearly two when Simon was born, exactly the age when sibling jealousy can be its greatest. Furthermore, we knew that Alex simply did not like other children. We weren't sure how that would play out with one actually living in the house.

Nanette's due date came and went. It was late August and she was heavy, hot, and impatient. She was about a week overdue when she told her mother to come up to Ithaca from Fort Lauderdale. We were new in town and didn't have friends that we could leave Alex with if we had to dash to the hospital. Having Nanette's mother around would be a big help. She could only stay a week or two, but we figured the baby was coming any day now.

Nanette's mother arrived, but the baby did not. We played with Alex, went shopping, and sat around and looked at each other.

"Let's go for a hike," suggested Nanette.

"What?" I asked.

"Exercise brings on labor, and I want this baby to come out already."

The three of us drove a few miles to Tremain State Park and walked along the stone path by a series of waterfalls. Some of the rock formations looked like they were fashioned by a stone mason, complete with near perpendicular lines. By the end of the day there was still no hint of a contraction. We felt our life was on hold.

Finally, after a few days, when we were just starting to get testy, Nanette felt the first signs of labor. It was early in the morning, before sunrise. We grabbed our things and drove across town to the hospital situated high on a hill overlooking Lake Cayuga. Once there we were told to go home. It was the very early stages of labor. The nurses felt that the baby wouldn't be born for hours, and we lived only 30 minutes from the hospital.

"The baby's coming quickly," said Nanette.

The nurses disagreed. "Come back in a few hours," they said, "Why wait here?"

"By time I get home, I'm going to have to turn around and come back."

"You should go home."

"I'll wait here." We didn't want anything to go wrong or to be rushed this time.

Shortly thereafter – in about the time it would have taken us to drive home, turn around, and get back to the hospital – Nanette entered the final stages of labor. Soon, Simon was born. He was overdue and so had lost some body fat, giving him an "overcooked" look. With little body fat, his features looked pronounced.

"Don't worry," said Nanette's mom, "Your brother does nose jobs."

But Simon was healthy and vigorous. No neonatal care, no emergency sutures, and no apprehensions. We could relax and enjoy the birth of our son. We were relieved, ecstatic, and worn out. And as he filled out, his nose assumed the proper proportions.

I manned the phones, and the nurses cleaned Simon off, put a little wool cap on his head, and sent him to the nursery.

"You know, Nanno, this is a lot more fun than when Alex was born."

"I know. I almost feel guilty thinking that."

Nanette lay back and relaxed. It was near midday and the light streamed into her hospital room window. She said, "I hope Alex takes this all in stride. Getting a new brother is a big deal. We're talking 'major life event'."

We didn't want Alex to feel like a second fiddle, so earlier in the week we purchased a big, red fire truck and hid it in the hall closet. Our plan was to give it to him when we got back to the house and make a big fuss over him. Being good yuppies, we had read plenty of articles about introducing a new sibling, and we wanted to do it right.

We pulled up to the house and went inside. Nanette held Simon, and I brandished the brand new, bright red fire truck.

"Hi Alex! We're home!"

We couldn't tell what Alex cared less about, Simon or the truck. He didn't acknowledge him. He didn't express excitement, annoyance, curiosity, or jealousy – and he never did. We were actually somewhat relieved. Here was a sibling problem that we wouldn't have to deal with.

There would be others.

As for now, though, I dove into my new job, still feeling a little awkward with my new title as "Professor Mont." I wanted to hang out with the graduate students who were more my age. But I had a doctorate, a house, two kids, and a wife. I pretty much had to admit I belonged with the adults.

7

Doors Opened and Closed

样

Raising Alex was exhausting. He sat on the floor befuddled by the toys in front of him. He chewed on toys like other children and threw them around but he never seemed to do anything creative with them. He constantly needed an adult to engage him in one of the few activities he found acceptable, such as reading, making Play-Doh letters, or stacking numbered cups.

Sometimes we'd take him to the playground. He loved being pushed in the swing, riding the merry-go-round or going down the slide. But we knew the good times were tenuous.

Alex would be contentedly riding a rocking horse attached to a large metal spring, boinging back and forth, dressed in overalls and sneaks. Another child would innocently approach. As long as she kept her distance Alex would continue rocking seemingly oblivious. As she got nearer, however, his concern would grow, and when she crossed some magic threshold – about fifteen feet – he would become agitated. Any nearer and he would cower behind our legs and scream. With a lot of cajoling and reassurance he could tolerate another child being nearby but direct interactions were out of the question. This went on until he was three years old.

Staying home alone with him all day, of course, was not an option. Nanette craved adult companionship, and we felt that the only way to get Alex to play with other kids was to try and expose him to them in safe settings.

Nanette joined a couple of playgroups, but they were often disasters – a screaming, scared little boy and an exasperated, isolated mother. And peppered throughout was the fear that we were pampering him, spoiling him, catering to what seemed to us to be ridiculous demands.

When Nanette went to playgroups, Alex screamed. He hid behind her in terror, or clung to her legs. He barely allowed her to have any sort of conversation and he did not let her relax. Nanette would look long-ingly at the other moms and kids. Her feelings would fluctuate between inadequacy and anger.

"Am I such a bad mom? Am I ruining my child? Why does he act like that? Sometimes I just want to say to him, Damn it, Alex, leave me alone for five minutes."

Playgroups were a source of comfort to some extent if for no other reason than that they provided Nanette with friends, but it hurt when it was clear that children were getting together one on one outside of playgroup but never with Alex. Other people rarely saw Alex when he wasn't agitated because anyone other than Nanette, Simon, and myself usually set him off.

Nanette was amazed at how little effort it seemed to take for other moms to play with their children. She'd ask, "OK, exactly what do you do with blocks?" The other moms were incredulous.

"Just play!"

"I set him down on the blanket with a basket of toys or a pile of blocks while I clean the kitchen."

We thought we were doing something wrong. Even as Alex got a little older and was nearing pre-school age he seemed at a loss to figure out how to entertain himself. Other mothers used to joke that Nanette was a super-mom because she was continually arranging various art projects, outings, and elaborate activities. Nanette said it was for survival. Without an activity Alex would quickly enter meltdown mode. He'd fill up with anxiety. He'd have fits.

Nanette would arise in the morning with a chasm of hours in front of her needing to be filled. After breakfast, she'd arrange art supplies on the table – maybe previously cut-out shapes to be glued onto paper plates or pipe cleaners. Once that activity had run its course, she'd read for an hour or two until lunch, after which she'd pull out a batch of home-made play dough she and Alex had made the night before to be fashioned into letters. Before long, Alex had the recipe memorized. As long as he was absorbed in one of these activities, Alex was content.

"Julia came by again today," Nanette said, sounding tired and a little sad.

"Oh great," I said sarcastically.

That was always difficult. Julia was a little girl who lived next door. In fact, she was the only other youngster in our tiny neighborhood. She was a year or two older than Alex, and an only child. When we moved in, she probably figured she had a playmate. When she saw Alex and Nanette in the backyard, she usually bopped over, wanting to play. She was a good kid but she never caught on that Alex had no use for her. Our hearts would sink as she snaked her way through the bushes that separated our yards. Inside of a minute, Alex would be a wreck.

"Hi, Julia. What have you got there?" asked Nanette.

"It's my new ball. Do you want to play with me?" She had long, straight, dark hair and large eyes, her belly still round from the last vestiges of baby fat.

Alex, who had been happily stacking cups or swinging for the past thirty minutes, grew tense. He looked like a kid with a bee flying around his head, hoping it wouldn't sting him.

"Alex, do you want to play with Julia?"

"NO!" He would cry. He wanted nothing more than to be left alone. Julia was resilient. She came by several times a week. Sometimes a few times a day. Alex continually rebuffed her.

"Why don't you just tell her to go home?" I asked.

"How can you tell a little four-year-old girl who wants to play to go away? She's trying to be nice. I tell her we're busy sometimes, but I can't hurt her feelings. Besides, it would be good for Alex if he learned to play with her."

As Alex's agitation grew, so did Nanette's. When Alex performed an activity he demanded no interruptions. Anything unexpected or any sudden transition from one activity to another would cause him no end of consternation. The activities that engaged Alex were limited, and Nanette would feel frustrated and bored. She was riddled with self-doubts. The advice of family and friends was to put him in a playpen or in his room.

"He needs to learn how to entertain himself," our parents would say. "You're spoiling him."

Intellectually that made sense, but something about it did not sit right with us. People argued we were soft and indulgent, but our gut feelings were that the advice was wrong. We tried it; sometimes for extended periods, but it failed to work. And in our hearts, we did not think that Alex was acting like a spoiled child. We honestly felt he did not know how to play – and that he needed to be taught. Playing seemed to come naturally to other children, but for Alex it was different.

On the other hand he seemed to learn some things effortlessly. He knew his letters by age two and was reading words by age three. He was counting at an amazingly tender age. People thought he was odd, but mostly they were impressed with how bright he was.

"Dan, do you see what he's doing with the chalk?"

Alex was sitting on our front steps, awkwardly scribbling on the concrete with a piece of thick, pink chalk.

"What?"

"Look at what he's writing. Am I nuts?"

I bent over Alex. Long wavy lines were traced out across the landing. With a little imagination, they looked like letters.

"Does that spell Daddy?" I asked. "That can't be."

"That's what I thought. But look, I think it does. He's not even three years old, Dan. He can barely control the chalk."

"Did you teach him how to spell Daddy?"

"No. I guess it's in one of his books, but…"

Even better than books and letters, Alex loved to count. Since he learned so easily I decided to teach him how to count by twos. "Teach" is an overstatement. It was more like I just suggested the idea to him and he took off with it. And it wasn't just memorization.

"Alex, now can you count by two starting from the number five?"

"five, seven, nine, eleven…"

"How about counting by threes starting from number one?"

"one, four, seven…"

He didn't even have the fine motor skills to write the numbers down, but pretty soon he was adding them together. And he did this without props. I didn't have to make little piles of four beans and two beans, push them together and then add them up. He took to numbers like a bird being launched from its nest.

He was afraid of other kids and often times high strung, but academically he was precocious. I was a professor. I knew plenty of socially odd but highly intelligent people. Maybe Alex was one of them.

Alex also had strange routines that had to be followed or he would get very upset. For example, he had to be the one to turn off the light or close a door. If he were not allowed to do so he would freak out. Wailing and stamping his feet, his face would turn crimson. The peculiar thing about these tantrums, though, was that you did not get a sense of anger from Alex, as much as you did one of panic.

After Simon was born (when Alex was almost two years old), Alex's need to open all doors became a serious problem. I can tell you from personal experience that when you have a toddler and a baby in a stroller and you are walking along downtown, *everyone* wants to open doors for you. Invariably, this would result in screams from Alex, belabored attempts on our part to explain that people were merely trying to be nice, and puzzled and disapproving looks from other people.

On nice days I sometimes took Alex and Simon to the downtown section of Ithaca, called the Commons. The Commons is about two blocks of quaint shops and restaurants blocked off to traffic. We'd watch street performers, or lounge on benches under trees or in a pavilion. When it wasn't crowded, we would play on a small playground. More often than not, we ran into people we knew because Ithaca is a small town.

With Alex, a trip there was like entering a minefield. I would be walking along, trying to time my arrival at doors to not coincide with other shoppers because, BOOM, Alex would explode when they opened the door for us. To prevent this from happening, I'd alternately zip along or slow down, simultaneously on the alert, BAM, for small children who elicited cries of anguish from Alex. And then, of course, off to the left would be an acquaintance. Should I ignore her? Wave? If I slowed down Alex would get very upset and agitated because as far as he was concerned I had aborted our activity for no apparent reason. And then, horror of horrors, someone might actually say hello to him or pat his head. KAPOW!

"Why did he say hello to me ?!!"

"It's OK, Alex, he was just being friendly."

"WHY DID HE SAY HELLO?!!"

"Shhh. Shhh. It's OK, we'll be going in a minute. I'll explain later."

Sometimes, Nanette and I would avoid places with lots of people. Navigating the minefield was not worth the strain. Moreover, I could not stand the looks people gave me. Oh, those looks.

"What a spoiled brat," eyes would flash.

"A little proper parenting would set that boy right," said a curled lip.

"What's wrong with him?" chimed in a pair of eyebrows.

Worst of all, part of me worried that they were right. Other parents did not seem to alter their lives as much as we did. Other parents did not treat situations as gingerly or with as much forethought. Most importantly, other children seemed more relaxed and more able to cope with the world and enjoy it.

The "look" followed us everywhere. Every time Alex screamed or cried or threw a tantrum for seemingly no apparent reason, or when we entered one of our lengthy and complex explanations that seemed to calm him down. For example, when a waiter would place a glass of water in front of him. You see, he hadn't ordered it. Or every time someone touched him or asked him his name. He was outraged that people felt they had the right to try to engage him without his permission. Alex wanted no contact with anyone outside the family. Other people were an annoyance – worse than an annoyance. They were a source of terrifying unpredictability. He simply did not understand anybody's motivation for doing anything, or what their intentions were.

Alex needed truckloads of explanations. He needed everything just so. An unexpected transition from one activity to the next would set him off. Anything the least bit unpredictable would put him on edge. Were we coddling him? It didn't feel that way. He was just very sensitive, we thought.

Sensitive. That's what the first professional we contacted told us. Nanette went to a child psychologist when Alex was not yet two years old. She explained her concerns about Alex's near phobia of other children.

"Some children are just more sensitive than others," the therapist explained. "Alex probably had a bad experience with another child in playgroup when you weren't looking. He's generalized that to all children. You simply have to slowly reintroduce him to other children in gradual steps." She thought there was no need for concern.

"He's just shy like his father. He's the kind of kid you'll need to put in karate."

The advice seemed to make sense. It worked slowly, at least to the extent that over the next year his fear of children softened to concern until it eventually reached tolerance. That is, until the child did something unexpected or something that violated Alex's rules of interaction.

Amazingly, however, the psychologist never asked to see Alex. These pronouncements were made without any contact with our son. It stuns me now to think that we did not follow up further at that point. In fact, I find it rather embarrassing. I suppose if he hadn't been our first child, I would have had enough of a frame of reference to realize things were not that simple. Maybe I just wanted to wish the problems away.

Alex was a beautiful boy. He had a cherubic face with large bluish-gray eyes, framed along the top by bangs of bright blonde hair. When he was relaxed, his skin was smooth and his features delicate. When he was happy, he had a huge, ingratiating smile. Like all children, he had that indefinable air that made you want to tousle his hair or pick him up or make him laugh.

But approach Alex in any way he did not expect or approve of and he was a boy transformed. His face would redden, the muscles under his skin would tighten, and his body, once soft like a teddy bear, would stiffen. At first the agitation would seem like anger. His voice would get high, strained, and loud. He'd yell and his eyes would water. What made his countenance different from those of other children getting upset, I think, would be this look of concern mixed with indignation. He seemed afraid, offended, and if the situation was not rectified he'd progress to panic and almost helplessness. He'd scream and rant and look at me, as if to say, "Why? Why, Dad? What do they want from me? Why can't they just GET THE HELL OUT OF HERE!"

Alex's hang-ups had a huge effect on our lives. Whenever we were out in public or even when a neighbor came over to the house there was an undercurrent of tension, waiting for the next explosion. Even vacations were affected.

A research paper of mine was accepted at a conference in Ottawa and Nanette thought it would be fun to turn the trip into a mini-vacation. We loaded up the kids and all their accoutrements into our Taurus wagon and drove up to Ottawa. While I was at the conference Nanette visited a children's museum, walked along the river, and basically catered to the children.

"Are you attending more meetings today?"

"No, I can skip today. What do you want to do?"

"I'd love to tour the Parliament building, if the kids will let us."

"Why not? We should be able to do something for ourselves. It won't be so terrible."

"What dream world are you living in?"

"Let's do it." I said. "You almost never get a chance to do anything for yourself."

"OK, but if Alex has a meltdown, you can deal with him."

"I'll entertain him. You push Simon. There will be things to look at."

We walked the few blocks to the Parliament building, and joined a tour. There were other children. They made noise. We had to stop when the tour guide stopped. For Alex, it was a nightmare, but we were determined to get to the end of that damn tour come hell or high water. I worked as hard as I could to calm Alex and entertain him. I counted. I added. I desperately tried to keep him from screaming. I was doing a pretty good job actually, trailing a little way behind the group, when we came to a large room with an electric door.

Alex lit up. I cringed. He wanted to open the door. The door had an electric eye and opened automatically whenever anyone approached it.

"Wait, Alex, please wait. After everyone is inside and the door shuts we can go and open it."

The tour group filed in and then I set Alex down on the floor so he could open the door. Once inside, I stayed in the back. Alex would have been perfectly content to immediately turn around and walk out the door, but I wanted to hear at least a little of the tour guide's spiel. After a short while it was clear the tour group was about to turn around and walk out of the room. I started moving towards the door. Out of the corner of my eye I saw a young girl – maybe eight or nine years old – making a beeline to the door. Quickly, I dodged in front of her, put my leg out to the side to block her path as I swooped Alex off of my shoulders and shoved him in front of me towards the door. As I did this – and received the appropriate opprobrium from my fellow tourists – somebody entered the room from the hallway, opening the God forsaken door. Alex stood there waiting for the door to shut all the way as I blocked off the people behind me. He didn't want to open it until he was sure it was completely closed. I could sense the growing annoyance from the other tourists.

I yelled, "Alex, just open the door already!" and gave him a push. He left the room but he had not opened the door exactly as he had wished. He started to cry but at least not wail. A staff person in the hallway came up to us, "Are you OK, little boy?" Now, Alex wailed. I left the tour. Nanette finished it, but it was hardly a victory.

When Alex was diagnosed as autistic at age three and a half, we were given a bibliography of books aimed at parents. One of these was entitled *Please Don't Say Hello*[*]. When I read that title my throat clutched and my eyes grew hot with tears. How can I explain that feeling? How could somebody else know what we were going through? You mean, other children like Alex existed? Maybe we weren't crazy. Maybe we

---

*   Gold, P-T. (1975) *Please Don't Say Hello.* New York: Human Sciences Press.

weren't bad parents. Maybe we could help our son learn to get along in the world.

After the diagnosis, the "look" no longer made me feel insecure as a parent or embarrassed. Instead it alternately infuriated me or just made me feel tired. Tired with all the countless efforts of trying to explain Alex to family, friends, and professionals. Now I barely notice it, and I hope I never give it out myself. But I still marvel when I see a small child and wink at them or make a funny face and they laugh.

8

"You Want to Do It!"

CB

The first time Alex said, "Daddy," I was in heaven. Nanette had brought him up to the building where I had my graduate student office. She was pushing his juice-stained stroller down the hall and he was walking beside it, not quite two years old. It was late in the afternoon, and the hall was nearly empty. I saw them from about thirty feet away and loudly said, "Hi Alex!"

"Daddy!" Alex shouted, and started clumsily running down the hall towards me. He had said "Daddy" a few times before but never so clearly and with so much enthusiasm. I ran to meet him and scooped him up.

"Hey, big guy! Did you come to see Daddy?"

The thought of having a conversation with Alex thrilled me. Even if all we could discuss was the color of his toys.

Alex's speech development, though, was unusual for a normal child. Alex never cooed or babbled. He never tried to imitate sounds that we made. He barely made any sounds at all when he was a baby except for crying and occasional laughing. By the time he was 18 months old he still had not spoken. This was getting to be late but was still not unreasonably so. Our doctor told us if he did not start talking by the age of two we should go to a speech pathologist.

At around 20 months, we were sitting in the children's section of the public library. In the middle of the room, surrounded by bookcases and cloth wall hangings in earth tones, was a Brio train set laid out on a long, low table. A track circuit made its way around the table, lined with little wooden buildings, trees, and people. Alex enjoyed connecting the cars on the tracks. Trains fascinated him. One of his favorite books at the time chronicled a train ride through small towns and the countryside. It rhymed, naturally, and the whole family had it memorized.

Alex, dressed in light-blue corduroy overalls and a red shirt, a tousle of platinum blonde hair spilling over into his eyes, methodically attached and reattached the brightly colored cars. This activity was one of the few playful things he did with toys, though he never embellished it with anything resembling imaginative play.

Eventually it was time to leave. I got up out of my bean bag chair, walked over to Alex and told him we needed to get going. After about the third time of trying to get his attention, he said, "No!" I thought, "Yes! He actually used a word."

Over the next few months "no" was followed by a growing list of words. We relaxed and even chuckled at ourselves. We were typical overanxious first-time parents.

Slowly, however, we began noticing funny aspects of Alex's use of language.

All children start off by reversing their pronouns. They say, "You want a cookie" when they mean "I want a cookie," or "Me do it" when they want you to do it. That is a natural enough mistake. Whenever people direct their speech at a child, they refer to him or her as "you." If they want the child to hand them something they say "Give it to me" with "me" meaning the person speaking.

Most children quickly infer that "me" means the speaker and "you" refers to the person being spoken to. Correcting this pronoun reversal problem can take a few days, a few weeks or even a couple of months. For Alex it took over two years.

The parenting books we read advised letting language develop naturally. Parents, they said, should not constantly correct a child's grammar. That would make them self-conscious and limit their use of language. So at first, we ignored Alex's confusion with pronouns for the most part. In the end, though, the only way we could help him to straighten out his pronouns was through numerous belabored and explicit explanations.

"Alex, when Daddy says, 'Give it to me,' the word 'me' means Daddy because it is Daddy saying 'me.' If Alex says 'me' then 'me' means Alex."

I would have to refer to myself as "Daddy," that is, in the third person, because otherwise Alex would not be sure whom I was talking about. Nanette and I must have gone through similar explanations thousands of times before Alex finally worked everything out.

I struggled to maintain my patience. "Why doesn't he understand this? He learns other things so fast."

"Yeah, it can't be a cognitive problem. He's so smart."

We kept at it.

In the meantime, Alex's pronoun reversal only reinforced the frustration he felt interacting with people other than Nanette and myself. People were invariably confused about what he was saying. He went into a rage one day when a parent of a classmate would not let him open the refrigerator door to get a snack even though Alex (then three years old) was insisting that "You open the door!" The resulting scene resembled an Abbot and Costello routine.

"You open the door!"

"OK, honey, I'll open the refrigerator and get you a snack."

Screams. The door is shut.

"No. *You* open it!"

"OK. You want me to open it?"

"Yes. You open it."

"OK." The door opens. Screams. Tears. Frustrated rage. Adult befuddlement. "What am I doing wrong?"

Another oddity of Alex's speech was that he often parroted back what was said to him – especially if it was a question.

"What does Alex want for breakfast?"

"Alex want for breakfast."

"Right. *What* does Alex want for breakfast."

"Want for breakfast."

"Alex, will you answer the question? What do you want for breakfast?"

"Want for breakfast."

"For Christ's sake! Just tell me! Do you want Cheerios?"

"You want Cheerios."

"Alex wants cheerios?"

"Yes."

"Because when Daddy is talking to Alex and Daddy says 'you' then Daddy means Alex."

He wanted Cheerios. I wanted to pull my hair out. This was constant. It was unceasing.

His echolalia – for that is the technical term for this kind of repetition – manifested itself in more subtle forms, as well. For example, Alex never made any mistakes with verb tense or word usage. Most children do. It is a normal part of speech development. They say things like, "I goed to the store" instead of "I went to the store." They generalize the English language past tense form "ed" to irregular verbs that have different conjugations. Alex never made generalizations like that because he only repeated things he had already heard. In fact, he didn't create a truly original sentence until he was in kindergarten. Up until that point he only rearranged sentences and sentence fragments that he had heard or read. This method allowed him to communicate what he wanted to express. Even now, at age 11, his language can sound stilted.

Alex was a precocious reader, so combined with his echolalia and pronoun reversal his speech was often not intelligible to the uninitiated. For example, at age three or four, if he saw a vending machine out of the corner of his eye and he wanted some candy he would say, "You insert a coin in this slot."

Alex lacks the ability to infer the subtle structure of human communication. This disability goes beyond his abilities to generalize language. For instance, Alex had difficulty knowing when someone was speaking to him as opposed to somebody else who was in earshot. He would become agitated if he did not know the answer to a question that I was actually posing not to him but to Nanette.

"Be careful, this is hot," I said, passing a steaming pot of spaghetti to Nanette.

"What?" asked Alex.

"I'm not talking to you, Alex. I'm handing the spaghetti to Mommy and I'm talking about the pot. OK? So...Nanette...did you hear about the commotion up on campus today?"

"Hear what?" asked Alex, getting agitated.

"Alex. I was talking to Mommy. I said, 'Nanette.' When I say 'Nanette' that...OH! Look out, you're spilling that!"

"Don't yell at me!" screams Alex.

"I'm not yelling at you!" I say, now yelling. "You're not spilling anything, OK? Simon is...just be quiet!"

Tears from Alex. Frustration from myself.

I found myself telling my child who was incapable of holding a conversation to shut up. I was keyed up from work, filled with the day's news, just wanting to converse with Nanette and relax. But my feelings were conflicted. I also wanted to teach my son to talk and hold a conversation – he never seemed to be in synch with language and each misunderstanding was an opportunity to teach him something. The constant explanations, though, wound me in knots.

"You see, Alex, when Daddy says 'you', then I'm referring to you – I mean Alex. I mean that Daddy means Alex...oh just drink the damn juice."

"Don't yell at him."

"I'm not yelling."

"You just told him to drink the damn juice."

"But I wasn't yelling. I'm just sick and tired of the 'me means me and you means you' stuff."

"How else will he learn?"

"I don't know. He's not learning now. Do you know how many times we've been through this? Literally? Hundreds, I'd say thousands of times."

There were other problems, too – more complex ones.

How do you know in a room full of people that someone is speaking to you? Clearly you read both verbal and non-verbal cues.

Most of the time you interpret them without even being aware of what you are doing. We had to provide Alex with a set of rules he could use to determine if he was the one being spoken to.

Our first rule was, "Someone is not speaking to you unless they are looking at you." The inadequacy of this rule was discovered quickly.

"Alex, answer me, please, I'm talking to you."

"But you're not looking at me!"

"Alex, I'm driving a car," I'd say, trying to stay calm, "In a car, someone in the front seat may not be looking at you, especially if they are driving and need to see where they are going."

Here's another rule. Someone is speaking to you if they start off by using your name. For example, "Alex, let's go outside and play."

Cut to the next scene.

"Alex needs some new socks. Could you pick some up at the supermarket?"

Eventually, we came up with a list of rules that although not foolproof could explain practically all situations. However, it was several months of explanations like...

"Alex, listen to me. I wasn't talking to you. I was looking at Simon and talking about applesauce on his face. You don't have any applesauce. Therefore, I wasn't talking about you."

...before he finally got it.

We were both frazzled and baffled. How could Alex be smart enough to understand our explanations and dense enough not to pick up on the obvious?

He could not infer anything from the context of a conversation. Time after time, we had to break down social rules – often using flow charts or lists – in order to help Alex learn how to deal with some social phenomenon. Alex, for example, could not deal with the amount of noise Simon generated. He would cry in frustration whenever Simon was being moderately loud. If Alex were particularly edgy even the slightest sounds would bring an instant outburst. He had no ability to cope with the situation. We tried outlining his options by posting flow charts on the wall. Their helpfulness varied by situation but they were generally a calming influence. They gave him a frame of reference.

Alex has always had to have everything explained to him at length. Every detail of every situation has to be articulated to a logical exactitude that surpasses the best written Supreme Court decisions. Various experts have explained the reason behind this need to us. The heart of the matter lies at the way Alex learns. He does not make inferences well, especially social ones, although he has an exceptionally keen mind for deduction and analytical pursuits. In fact, he isn't even able to determine what social rules are the important ones to focus on. For example, for an extended period he was fixated on how you know whether to seat yourself upon entering a restaurant or wait to be seated. He approached this problem gravely, and wanted to know the "rules." He attached a great importance to it. If we entered a restaurant without a sign he would become very concerned. We thought we had this one figured out.

"If there is no sign then you only seat yourself if you need to go to the counter to get the food yourself." Like with McDonald's or Burger King.

That worked fine until we went to a Sunday brunch buffet.

The thing is, when we came across an exception (and every custom or rule of behavior is riddled with them) Alex seemed betrayed. He desperately wanted the world to be structured – to make sense – otherwise the world descends into chaos. And chaos meant meltdown and meltdown sometimes drove us to the breaking point.

At night we lay in bed with the lights off and talked.

"Did you believe that car thing?" asked Nanette.

"What? The 'you can't be talking to me because you're not looking at me'?"

"Unbelievable."

"I almost decided to throw in the towel and drive over a cliff right then and there. It's like a twist on that Robert De Niro movie, 'Taxi Driver' – Talkin' to you? Yeah, I'm talkin' to you. Who the *hell* do you *think* I'm talkin' to?"

"I'm sorry. I wasn't listening. Were you talking to me?" said Nanette, laughing.

"Yes. When we're lying in bed worried about Alex, and I'm wringing my pillow, then, yes, I am talking to you."

9

Taking Turns

CB

We were constantly on the prowl for ways to amuse Alex, for our own sanity as much as for his sake. So when a friend invited us to a Discovery Toys party, we jumped at the chance. We drove out to our friends' house and piled into the living room with a few other sets of parents, some of whom had brought their children along. Brightly colored toys were displayed on a table along with some games – all designed to stimulate or educate your child. At that point we weren't all that interested in educate, we were searching for "entertain" – or at least, "occupy."

We bought a few things. We are toy-aholics. Two of the most successful toys we got were cups numbered one to ten that stacked inside each other, and a contraption with colored balls and a hammer. You banged one of the rubber balls through a hole and watched it roll down a series of ramps where it would inevitably be snatched up by a pudgy hand, only to be rammed through again and again.

We can't remember exactly why, but we also decided to buy a board game. Even though Alex was only two and supposedly too young to play, we thought he'd like it. It was a shapes game. You rolled a six-sided die that had different shapes on each face. If you rolled a circle, for instance, you placed a circle on a picture composed of the same shapes that appeared on the die. The circles were the wheels of a car, a rectangle was the chassis, and so forth. The first person to completely cover his or her picture was the winner.

The first time Alex played this game he practically collapsed with laughter. The tension melted from his face and body. Never had I seen him so relaxed. It was wonderful to behold. This poor little boy always seemed on edge – tied up in knots. Watching his anxiety disappear was like removing a weight from my chest.

Board games saved our lives, but it was like Dr Seuss all over again. He would play for hours. We did not have to scurry around trying to create or preserve structure or routine all day long. It was hand delivered to us. On the other hand, I started having dreams of continually rolling dice.

Most two-year-olds don't play board games. Most three-year-olds don't, either. Alex was playing the shapes game hours on end when he barely had the coordination to do what was physically required. He couldn't even pronounce the names of the shapes properly. We used to laugh whenever his die came up with a semi-circle on it. His face would light up and he'd shout, "You got a Hemi-hircle!" Win or lose, he was in heaven.

Later, after Alex was diagnosed and I began reading books about high-functioning autistics, I came across a book written by an autistic man named Sean Barron and his mother.* A chapter of that book helped me understand why Alex probably loved and continues to love games.

When Sean was a young boy one of the joys of his life was being driven down dead-end streets. Whenever his family would pass one while travelling around town in their car, he would get hysterical if they refused to turn and follow the street to its end. His desire was intense and inexplicable to his parents. His mother reports rearranging her driving routes to avoid dead-end street signs. That strategy wasted less time than turning down each and every dead-end street, and avoided the fits that would occur if she did not.

*   Barron, J. (1992) *There's a Boy in Here.* New York: Simon and Schuster

When Sean got older he was able to explain his desire. The world, thought Sean, was a confusing place. Waves of information were constantly assaulting him and it all came too fast and dense for him to absorb. When he saw a dead-end street, however, he knew – with certainty – that the road ended. With that knowledge he could screen out other uncertainties and focus on how the road would end. Would there be a fence? A cul de sac? A wall? The safety and security of knowing that it *would* end, enabled him to enjoy the uncertainty of exactly *how* it would end. He could relax and enjoy the unexpected because the randomness of life, in this instance at least, was well contained.

Alex's love of board games, I believe, stems from the same phenomena. The world is a confusing and overwhelming place but the rules of a board game are well defined. You know when it is your turn. You know exactly what to do. You can sit back and enjoy the surprises and random events because the outcomes are bounded. Alex was never as at ease as when he played his games.

As we tired of various board games we bought new ones – not so much for Alex who can play a favorite game ad infinitum, but for our own sanity. Alex now has dozens and dozens of board games, card games, dice games, etc. His extra-wide closet is stacked floor to ceiling with games, and he knows a wide variety of pencil and paper games, as well. Moreover, he has modified many of them to make them more interesting and complex. Alex can be quite creative, but only within the confines of well-defined rules. For example, he has invented numerous ways of playing tic-tac-toe, some of which are quite challenging. One version uses a conventional three-by-three board but when placing your "X" or "O" you have to use gravity – that is, the "X" or "O" must rest either on the bottom level or on another letter. Another version places a tic-tac-toe board within each square of a larger tic-tac-toe board. You must win a small board in order to place a large "X" or "O" in the larger board. This can be played with "local" gravity, in other words each little board has gravity, or "global" gravity, meaning you cannot place an "X" or "O" into a small tic-tac-toe board until the mini-games of tic-tac-toe in the large squares underneath it are filled. A more complicated version of this game allows for two-way gravity – you can "drop" an "X" or "O" onto the board and have it fall either from top to bottom, or from left to right.

Nanette and I joke that we should start a newsletter reviewing games for kids and parents to make use of our store of knowledge. Or at least put out a volume entitled "101 Ways to Play Tic-Tac-Toe."

10

"I Know, Mom, I Know"

❀

"We could really use a play structure out back," said Nanette. "The boys would get a lot of use out of it."

"OK. Do you want to go shopping for one today?"

"I want to build one."

"What?!"

"They have kits."

"Kits? But...isn't that a lot of work?"

"I'm going stir crazy. Besides, I like building things. It'll give me something productive to do."

"But I thought you were exhausted."

"This is a totally different thing. I'll build it while the kids are napping."

"That's not how I'd spend my free time, but..."

"Well, I'm building one."

A few weeks later the playground company dropped off stacks of uncut, pressure-treated wood, bags of bolts and other hardware, and the makings of an enclosed, spiral slide in our driveway. Nanette set up a work station in the garage and started cutting wood. I helped her carry the heavier pieces to a flat area behind our house.

Slowly, a playhouse, slide, and monkey bars materialized at the back of our yard. Nanette would take out her frustrations on the wood.

Her hair back in a ponytail, with nails in her mouth, she'd pound together the structure. One of the few things – thank heavens – that Simon and Alex cooperated on was naptime. Over the course of several months and dozens of naps, Nanette sawed, sanded, hammered, and bolted together a formidable play structure. I chipped in occasionally when two sets of hands were needed and did some token hammering. After a few weeks, Nanette attached the multi-colored tarp to the top of the playhouse and it was completed.

The boys used the structure constantly and Nanette felt proud and productive. Also, she was determined to be a positive role model for the boys; she was a stay-at-home mom but she didn't want them to develop a stereotypical image of women.

One day, however, a few months later when a visitor remarked on what a great play structure we had, Simon smiled, pointed to it, and said, "My Daddy made that!"

Nanette's expression – anger, amusement, and disbelief – defies description. The best laid plans. I made sure to constantly reinforce that Mommy built that, and had Simon accompany me on expeditions to buy Nanette's birthday and Mother's Day presents – you know, the usual things, like belt sanders and circular saws. She went on to make a play table and bookcase.

Around this time, when Alex was about three, my parents came up to Ithaca for a visit. It was a beautiful day, so we drove over to a local playground. Bob Leathers, a world renowned designer of playground structures, lives in Ithaca, so the town is filled with great castle-like playgrounds. We went to one just a couple miles from our house.

I was attempting to coax Alex down a slide. The playground was a labyrinth of tunnels and bridges, made of wood and tires and large chains. Children swarmed up ladders, jumped across gaps, bounced on bridges, and swung from apparatus to apparatus. By this point, Alex was no longer terrified by other children; they were merely a nuisance.

Of course I wanted my parents to be impressed by Alex. He was three years old. I also wanted to show them that I was a good parent. They had heard some of my concerns about Alex, and I knew they thought Nanette and I were overly doting.

"Alex, it's your turn to go down the slide."

"You want him to go away."

I took a breath. "Alex, that boy isn't in the way. You won't hit him if you slide down."

"You want him to go away!"

"Alex, you can't wait until everything is perfect. Other children want their turns. You need to slide down now. That boy is not that close to the slide. I can't just tell him to move. This playground is for everybody."

Another child yells. "Go down the slide!"

"Come on, Alex!" I said between clenched teeth.

All around me children were playing and laughing, mingling with and around each other with ease. Alex was perched atop the slide, holding up the line. Out of the corner of my eye I saw my mother sitting on a bench, looking at me. She seemed worried. I could tell she disapproved but was reticent about speaking to me. I was embarrassed, but I was worried, too. All I wanted in the world at that moment was for Alex to go down that slide. Why couldn't he play like the other kids? I tried to talk calmly but what I really wanted to do was just push him down the slide. I knew that was wrong. I knew that would make him scream. I also knew the only way to get him to go down by himself was to finish my lengthy dissertation on the subject of slides, turn taking, and why other children were allowed on the playground. Afterwards, I walked over to my mother. I was afraid I might be on the receiving end of a lecture.

"Daniel," my mom said, "You shouldn't need to go through all that."

"I know, Mom." I didn't want to hear it.

"Just tell him to go down the slide and walk away."

"I know, Mom."

"That's what I always did with you."

"I know, Mom, but it won't work. He needs the explanations. I don't know why he needs them, but he does. I'm doing the best I can."

"I know, Daniel. I know."

In a way my mother did know what I was going through. My younger sister, Diane, had a very difficult childhood. She had severe emotional problems, was prone to tantrums, outbursts, and at times near uncontrollable behavior. She had difficulties learning in school, and had very few friends. She was an unhappy child, hounded mercilessly at school and forced, at times, to retreat into her own fantasies and obsessions.

The daily strain of raising Diane was enormous. There was the fear of outbursts, but on a deeper level there were the constant worries about her future. Would she be able to support herself? Would the lack of judgement that put her in one precarious predicament after another lead to some tragedy? Were my parents taking the right steps in helping her?

Growing up, I saw the toll it took on my mother and father. Diane was one of the few things they argued about. She dominated every discussion. She had a disproportionate impact on every facet of our family life from dinnertime to vacations. My older sister, Debbie, and I would talk about the inevitable day when she would become our responsibility.

As it turned out, Diane – through a degree of resiliency and resolve that deserves its own book – has pulled herself together and lives independently. She has conquered most of her problems and is building a life for herself.

But my mom, sitting on that bench by the playground, had an inkling that something might be seriously wrong. I think that scared her. I think she was concerned we were worsening the situation.

"You don't think you're spoiling him?" she asked.

"No, I don't. I don't want to tell him to just 'do this'. I think it's a good idea to give him an explanation."

"OK."

She wasn't convinced.

"I'll tell you one thing," I thought to myself, "I'm going to be a lot more consistent with Alex than you were with Diane. I mean, don't you criticize me. You're not with him every day!"

Then I'd catch myself.

"That's brilliant, Dan," I thought. "Like there's a comparison. Like you could've done any better than she did."

"Come on, Alex," I said aloud, trying not to plead. "Just slide down the slide."

"Please," I thought, "What's the big deal? Just slide down the God damn slide."

11

My Parents

CB

My parents were both born in Newark, New Jersey. My father grew up during the Great Depression and spent his whole childhood in poverty. His father worked irregularly and the family didn't have much. He learned responsibility early, having various jobs from the time he was in elementary school with little time for homework.

One summer he was sent away to a camp for economically disadvantaged city kids. They called it a relief camp. His strongest memory was not the other children or the games or activities but the fact that he could have as much milk or orange juice as he wanted. The more he drank, the more it flowed.

"I had this one friend. His name was Harvey," said my dad. "I was so jealous of him because whenever we went to his house his mother would give him a tall, cold glass of tomato juice. She never gave me anything. I had to sit and watch Harvey drink that juice. It looked so good I could practically taste it. But when I went to camp I could have as much as I wanted."

The day after he came home he went into the kitchen for breakfast and poured himself a glass of milk. After finishing it, he asked for more. The bottle was empty. His mother – who immigrated from the Ukraine as a teenager with her five brothers and a father who died in an accident shortly after arriving in America – went to the cabinet. She stood up on a chair and reached for the jar of emergency change.

"I was never more ashamed of myself," my dad recalled. "How dare I ask for more? She took down that jar and counted out the pennies."

"Please Ma," my dad said, "I don't want any more."

"Yes, you do," said his mother. "Go down to the store and buy another quart of milk."

My dad shakes his head when he tells the story.

"It was the worst milk I ever drank."

My mother didn't grow up that poor, but money was not plentiful either. Her father ran a dry-cleaning store in Irvington, the last of several ventures. When my mom graduated high school in 1955 she was accepted into college. No one in her family had ever graduated from college, and it was still unusual for women to attend.

"I remember going down to visit the campus at Trenton State," she would recount. "It was so exciting."

I could see the girlish wonder and pride still lurking in her eyes.

"But my father told me I couldn't go. He didn't have the money and he said that girls didn't need to go to college anyway."

"Your mom is a real smart cookie," my dad would say. "No telling what she could've done if she went to college."

"My Uncle Max offered to pay, but my father was too proud to take it, I guess."

"You're going to get married anyway," said my grandfather. "Why waste the time going to school?"

Under her high school yearbook picture it says she aspired to be an accountant. Instead, she got a bookkeeping job in New York City, and commuted from Elizabeth, New Jersey to Penn Station each morning by train.

My parents met at a Hadassah dance. It was love at first sight for my father; it took my mom a little longer. They were married in 1957 at a big Jewish wedding. My mother's parents sold their house to my mom and dad and moved into a trailer. Finances were tight.

My parents had a wonderful marriage but the early years were tough. My dad worked two jobs and when my older sister Debbie was born in 1959 my mother quit working and ran a laundry in their basement. My father dropped off and picked up laundry on his way to and from work. I came along two years later.

By the time my younger sister, Diane, was born in 1966, the laundry business was no longer needed. My father got a big promotion a few years later and we moved to Highland Park, New Jersey in order to get away from an increasingly deteriorating school system. My mother cried when she left her old neighborhood and the friends she'd known most of her life. For a few years afterwards we traveled to Elizabeth regularly to visit those friends. Eventually those trips petered out.

A couple of years after we moved, when I was in fifth grade and Debbie and Diane were in seventh grade and kindergarten, my father got very sick and was hospitalized for a few months. He lost his job and we almost lost our house. I didn't know how close we came to being on the street until I was a grown man. In fact, I remember fifth grade as being a particularly happy one. My mother worked hard to make us think nothing was wrong.

Once when I came home from college, my mom let me borrow the car as long as I would drop her and Diane off at Diane's therapist, Dr Goldstein, and then pick them up later. On the way home I saw that her eyes were red.

"Are you OK?"

"Yes. I'm fine."

"Really?"

"Actually, I feel a lot better."

"What do you mean?" Something was up.

She paused. "Diane didn't have her session today."

"Why?"

"I'll tell you when we get home."

I pulled into the driveway. Diane went to ride her bike. My mom and I went inside and she started chopping vegetables for dinner as I set the table.

"I had Diane's session."

"What?"

"Dr Goldstein took one look at me and asked me if I wanted to talk. He said it looked like I needed it more than Diane today."

"What did you talk about?"

"Oh, Daniel, don't take this the wrong way."

I got nervous. My mind raced to figure out if I had done something wrong. The other night I had argued with her. I told her that she was projecting her values onto me. I told her that different things were important to me than her – that I didn't want to grow up and live behind some white picket fence. I told her she didn't understand me at all. At that age I got angry and frustrated with her quite often – over politics, the way she treated Diane, and her attitudes about what I should be doing with my life.

"Was it something I did?"

"No." She took a deep breath. I could see she was struggling to decide if she should talk to me. "How can I say this? Lately I've caught myself getting jealous of you and Debbie. I hate myself for it."

I tried to interject something, but she waved me off.

"You travel, you go to college, you have your whole lives ahead of you. You're free. I'm so happy for you but I want some, too. I couldn't go to college. We haven't taken a vacation in what? Over ten years? I've never even been on a plane. Between Diane and bills…I don't know when I'm going to start living for me. Your father and I always say our day will come – you kids come first, but damn it, when is it my turn?"

"Mom—"

"You don't have to say anything. After talking to Dr Goldstein I realize I'm not really jealous of you. I just want something for myself."

My parents' plan was that once Diane was settled they would get down to doing all the things they wanted to do. Retirement would be the time they did things for themselves.

"But when you kids are happy and successful, well, then I know my life is successful."

12

A Team

Cʒ

How do children on a playground get in synch? How can they read each other enough to know what is acceptable? How do the rules of the game change so smoothly? It's breathtaking. And it seems all the more essentially human because much of the communicating that is taking place is never explicitly taught.

My other son, Simon, is not autistic. I am perfectly aware that children fight, children feel left out, and children get bored because there is "nothing" to do in a room full of playmates and toys. But you cannot comprehend the level of communication and cooperation that young children exhibit, almost intuitively, until you have a child that stands there looking like someone plucked from an aboriginal tribe and transported to the middle of Times Square.

Alex was nearing three years of age, and we both wanted him to start interacting more with other children and develop better social skills. It was clear to us, though, that Alex was not ready for a fully fledged immersion into the world of preschool. He was no longer phobic of other children, but he did not enjoy them. He also did not like being disengaged from any activity once he found something that captured his interest. Still, we believed it was important for his development to learn to be with other children. We thought preschool would be good for him. Plus, it would give Nanette some time alone with Simon.

We decided to look for a part-time situation. We selected a neighborhood school that had class half-days for three days a week. School could be stressful for him and we wanted to ease him into it. We were worried, but we hoped that by spending some time with other children, and also with adults experienced with small children, he might learn to get along better.

Most of our friends and family thought we were overly concerned. Alex was already showing signs of intellectual brilliance. He almost effortlessly taught himself to read by the time he was three years old. Nanette and I occasionally offered him some tidbits of information. Nanette would say, "If C-A-T spells cat, what does B-A-T spell?" Alex would answer, "Bat!" He was rarely wrong and rarely spent much time thinking about the answer.

The English language, however, quickly got us into trouble.

"If L-O-V-E spells love, what does D-O-V-E spell? What does M-O-V-E spell?"

The growing list of exceptions made us stop – he was barely three after all – but, before we knew it Alex had filled in the gaps and was reading. How he learned consonant blends and vowel combinations I'll never know.

Inconsistencies in the English language would sometimes infuriate him, though. For example, one time, when he was learning to read he asked me, "Daddy, what does R-A-N-G-E spell?"

I was surprised. This was a word I thought he knew.

"It spells range," I said.

"NO! It spells 'ringe'"

"What do you mean?"

"Well, O-R-A-N-G-E spells 'orange' so R-A-N-G-E must spell 'ringe'!"

He indignantly pointed to his plastic place mat, adorned with labeled fruits and other foods. We removed the offending place mat, but he kept up his determined effort to decode the English language, with no urging and little encouragement from us. We felt we would be overdoing it to stress out a child who was barely three, and he found the inconsistencies of English very annoying. We continued to read to him, but we tried to back off when it came to teaching him to read.

Alex felt betrayed by the English language. Here was something parading as a logical system with supposed rules and regularities but littered with exceptions and irregularities. He was hell bent on conquering this system. He dove into learning to read full force and attacked the irregularities like a pit bull. Luckily for him they are easier to learn than social interactions so he quickly mastered them.

Later, we discovered that precocious reading – called hyperlexia – is not uncommon with high-functioning autistic children. It seems contradictory to their difficulty with speech, but we have met several parents with similar stories. Alex also had a great facility with numbers – counting, adding, subtracting, and simple fractions. His abilities were very impressive for a three-year-old, which led a number of people to believe we were being hypersensitive to his problems.

"He is just developing unevenly. Things will straighten out by themselves. Don't worry so much."

"Exceptionally smart children are often socially backward."

"Relax and stop coddling him."

We wanted to believe them, but we had the nagging worry that his problems were more serious. Still, how could someone so bright have developmental problems?

We told the teachers about our concerns and explicitly asked them to let us know how he was doing. Of course, we sounded like typical first-time yuppie parents. We received some knowing smiles, and a few recitations of "There, there, not to worry." After several weeks we were told that he was immature but not "off the charts." Mostly we were told how bright he was.

"Do you know that he can read?"

"Yes we know he can read. Do you realize he never seems to interact with other children, and that he cries much of the time?"

Alex was not happy to go to school. Occasionally he would have tantrums but many kids have to adjust. With some trepidation we kept sending Alex to school. He was only going three half-days a week and we didn't think isolating him from other children was the answer to his problems. We were even beginning to think that he was starting to warm to the place. This warming, however, finally led to the incident which precipitated our getting Alex diagnosed.

Many autistic children do not like to be touched. Even as babies they often arch their backs and resist being cuddled. This was not the case with Alex. In fact, he has always been a very loving child. If anything, he has craved physical contact from people he is comfortable with. When he is ill at ease or with someone new, on the other hand, he despises contact.

Eventually, Alex started feeling more comfortable with the children at school. The school setting was becoming more familiar and after a few months he was not as anxious, or at least he wasn't continually anxious.

For most of the year, Alex had refused to participate in circle time. Circle time, as any parent knows, is that part of the day when the class sits together in a large circle, usually on the floor. The children sing songs or have a story read to them. Often it is the time for activities like show and tell. Alex generally had no use for these activities, and was not fond of sitting in such close proximity to the other children. He would usually wander about the room, straight-faced or even a little mopey, resisting efforts to include him. We felt it was a major step forward, therefore, when he eventually started joining the circle. The problem, however, was that his growing sense of comfort with the other children led to attempts on his part to reach out to them. He would try to sit in their laps and touch their faces. He would stroke their arms or legs. Getting right up into their faces, he would fall all over them. Three-year-olds touch each other a lot, but even for three-year-olds he was overstepping acceptable boundaries. The other children felt very uncomfortable.

Unfortunately no one told us this at first. Teachers are often taught that invading others' personal space and touching inappropriately are sometimes signs of sexual abuse. Added to Alex's general aura of unhappiness when he was at school and his associated social problems, his teachers began to have concerns. These teachers, instead of contacting us, decided to call Alex's pediatrician.

When they went behind our backs we felt violated. We were furious. Our roles as Alex's parents were being tossed aside. Besides, how could they think that of us? They had been dismissing our concerns and now they were questioning the most important thing in our lives, our relationship with our children.

It would have been easy to panic, or just overreact. I kept telling myself that they had not contacted any authorities. Maybe, I was being paranoid. Nanette wasn't so sure. She was livid. I wanted to avoid conflict. That's always my gut reaction – fight for what you want but be a peacemaker, a diplomat. Nanette was ready to explode.

Our reaction was compounded by my recent experience at work with the New York State child welfare system. At the time, I was conducting research on public policy relating to foster care and special needs adoption. I was only too well aware of the administrative miasma and pockets of officiousness that at times lurk within that system. And I had heard a number of horror stories of misunderstandings between parents and child welfare workers. Don't get me wrong; there are many wonderful caseworkers who devote their lives to children, but I'm sure even people within that system are familiar with the law, regulations, administrative procedures, and certain overbearing caseworkers that can make well-meaning parents' lives hell.

"Look, Nanno, they're just trying to protect Alex..."

"How can you be so fucking calm? Aren't you upset?"

"Yes. But what good is being upset? The question is..."

"We TOLD them we were concerned about his behavior, but, oh no, he was just a little 'immature.' They made me feel like an idiot for asking."

"I know. But even though they called the doctor, he called US. We'll get some professional help."

"How could they go behind our backs?"

"They only went to the doctor."

"That's NOT the point. We are his parents. I'm livid. Aren't you livid?"

We weren't sure what to do. Alex seemed different from other kids. How could we possibly go about explaining that when we weren't even quite sure we understood him ourselves? I shudder to think of the hoops we would have had to jump through if were made to deal with a call from Child Protective Services first instead of immediately pursuing the evaluative and treatment options we were able to choose on our own.

In the end, the difference between Nanette and me makes us a good team. Many situations arise where you need to fight or make a stand, even risk conflict. Nanette has the passion and the assertiveness to do that. On the other hand, there are times to take a deep breath and pick your battles – and to not put people on the defensive who are in a position to help you. I think our instincts complement each other well.

The only problem – for me, really – is my role as the steadier one. Often Nanette has said to me during times when things were particularly frustrating or when our worries were particularly intense, that she knew things weren't as bad as she felt because I wasn't so upset. She could calm herself by thinking she was overreacting.

I would lie in bed at night thinking it was my responsibility to hold things together. As we came to realize the severity of his problems, and later on after we heard the word "autism," it was hard to not think of the future with dread. Would he have friends? Would he fall in love? Would he have a normal life?

Nanette had the tougher job. She held things together on a daily basis, the nuts and bolts of life. She also constantly faced seeing other, normal children and Alex's interactions – or lack of interactions – with them. I had the respite of work. So when we lay in bed at night and she cried, I kept telling her to focus just on tomorrow, not years from now. And I kept assuring her that it wasn't all that bad. I wanted to cry, too, but I couldn't show that then.

Always, though, we tried to maintain focus first and foremost on our children. We're a team. That's why we very much wanted to be informed of any problems. That's why we had been pestering Alex's teachers for their opinions on his behavior in the first place.

13

Off the Charts

Cℬ

We drove down to Ellis Hollow Nursery School to meet with Alex's teachers. We were pissed. We were also a little apprehensive.

Ellis Hollow Nursery School was located in one small blue-gray building that doubled as the community center. It sat at the edge of several acres of open fields where the Ellis Hollow community held its fair in the summer, complete with home-baked pies and pony rides. There was a playground out back and a pool that was open in the summertime. The nursery school was one large room that took up most of the building.

When we arrived we parked in the gravel parking lot and went inside. We were greeted by Alex's teachers – two mothers from the neighborhood – and sat down in the too small chairs situated around a large table discolored by years of crayons and finger paints.

We were resolved not to express our anger at them for not coming to us first. Our primary concern was that everyone focus on what was best for Alex. We didn't want defensiveness getting in the way. Our anger grew, however, when his teachers presented us with a list of what they considered to be his problem behaviors:

Social Skills

1. No reaction to greetings in a.m., or leaving in p.m.

2. Doesn't interact with other children.

3. Will not accept help from other children.

4. Upset when another child tries to interact with him.

5. Prefers solitary activities to the point of isolating himself.

6. Doesn't seek or respond to comfort when upset.

7. No imaginative play.

8. Can't get his attention by saying his name, even difficult with physical contact.

9. Frequently have to insist on eye contact.

10. Frequent tantrums for insignificant things.

Speech

1. Reversal of pronouns (refers to self as "you").

2. Echoes back what is said to him.

3. Question-like melody in speech.

4. Can't carry on interactive conversation.

Daily Behavior Patterns

1. Upset by change in activities unless he chooses to do so.

2. Won't voluntarily come for circle time. Needs to be calmed daily.

3. Sometimes is upset when circle time is over.

4. Wants to start counting routines identically each day (examples: counting children, calendar)

This list does not paint a pleasant picture. This description does not portray a boy who is, in the previous words of his teachers, "a little immature but not off the charts."

Contrasting this list with their earlier reassurances angered me no end. Not being listened to by teachers and school officials is one of the most frustrating things we and our friends with special needs children have faced. Lack of communication is another. Time and again we have been told how important parental input and concern are and time and again we have been ignored and patronized. Our first experience was the scariest because of the specter of Child Protective Services, but unfortunately it has not been our last.

We decided to squelch that anger, though. Yelling at his teachers would only shift the focus off Alex, and we needed everybody's help. Besides, we felt guilty. We knew things weren't right. We had believed everyone's soothing words because we wanted to believe.

Clearly Alex needed help. We still were not sure, though, that he had a concrete developmental problem. A psychology professor whom I approached gave us her opinion that Alex might be autistic. She recommended that we go to Syracuse University to get him evaluated since they had a particularly good reputation in that area. At first we thought she was nuts, but when she showed us the list of traits used to diagnose autism, we made an appointment.

We felt fortunate that Syracuse was so close by. Living in a small town like Ithaca can be very disconcerting when you need special help. We were worried that resources we could find would be limited. One resource we did have, though, which was not a minor one, was Cornell University.

I called someone affiliated with the preschool program run by the Department of Human Development and Family Studies at Cornell University. She recommended we get Alex evaluated by the Special Children's Center, which was located in Ithaca. She assured me they saw a lot of children with special problems and that they took a very multidisciplinary approach to their evaluations. The problem with getting someone evaluated by a specialist – or by a person from one discipline – is that they are trained to look for only certain types of problems. The results you get from an evaluation by a psychiatrist, or a psychologist, or a speech therapist or an expert in autism or attention deficit disorder will by their very nature be different since they know different things and are used to looking for different sets of problems.

We called the Special Children's Center and decided to delay our appointment in Syracuse. We'd go to the autism experts, we thought, when we had a professional indication that autism might be the problem. And realistically, we thought, Alex couldn't be autistic.

14

The Evaluation

❧

The first day the Special Children's Center observed Alex, Nanette dropped him off at school, took a deep breath, and went back home with Simon. I set off to campus to teach a course on welfare policy. The two of us, though, could not shake from our minds the image of an evaluator following Alex about the classroom, scribbling notes, furrowing his brow, and concentrating his powers of observation on our little boy. Part of me thought this evaluator would come back to us with reassuring words and a few helpful suggestions, but part of me knew this was the beginning of a long process.

My class ended. I chatted with a few students, made my way back to my office, and closed the door. I looked at the clock. What was happening now? For one of the first times in my life, Alex felt really separate from me. Not that I wasn't close to him, but that he was truly a separate entity adrift in the sea – that in the final analysis I could never really know what was going on inside his head. It's a thought I have all the time now, but the first time it occurred to me it hit me hard.

I cleaned off my desk – the usual mountain of papers, books, and computer printouts – and took an early lunch. When Alex's school day was over, I called home.

"Well, what happened?" I asked.

"The Special Children's Center sent this guy, Andy. He's a special ed teacher. He's going to write a report and give it to us tomorrow and tell us if he recommends that Alex get a full-scale evaluation."

"What do you think?"

"Well, he said Alex seemed like a very sad little boy at school," said Nanette, trying to hold back the tears.

"Are you OK?"

"We should have done this sooner."

Mercifully, Andy's report came quickly. He had watched Alex at school, played one-on-one with him, and interviewed his teachers. Andy's report described a scared, lost, unhappy little child, adrift in the world and somehow set back from it. He spent most of the day distraught, wandering about the room, teary eyed. He made only the most fleeting connection with other children. My heart aches when I think back on reading that report for the first time. A myriad of emotions shoots every which way inside my head.

Andy met with us to review the report and recommend we schedule an evaluation at the Special Children's Center. He was a short, fit, sandy-haired man with a full mustache. The sort of person you'd expect to run into on a Sierra Club hike, dressed in jeans and work boots. He couldn't answer many questions, though. We'd have to wait for that. And waiting is not my strong point.

When we were alone, I took long looks at Alex. What was he thinking? What was he feeling? He was too young to have lines of consternation on his face. Why was he so afraid? Why was he so overwhelmed by the world? How could a boy his age have so much tumult going on inside him?

Alex could be happy. I knew that. Many times I'd seen him practically lose control over his body he was laughing so hard while playing some game. I have countless pictures of Alex laughing. I merely would have to spell his name incorrectly and he would break into hysterics.

"How do you spell Alex? A-L-E...Q?"

Alex would erupt into squeals of laughter. From our photo album you would think Alex was an ebullient child, not a child who alternated from serious to upset to no affect at all. But Alex never laughed at a puppet show or at a kid's joke. Stuffed animals might as well have been a lump of coal.

I would snuggle with Alex on the couch. He could be happy. He was a sad little boy but he could be happy.

Panic came from the thought that we had been dense and waited too long to take action. What were we thinking? Had we lost too much valuable time? He was only three and a half years old but early intervention is key in helping children with developmental problems. We had lost a year, we thought. We should have been searching out services a year earlier. Well, it wasn't productive dwelling on that. We scheduled an appointment for an evaluation.

When the day came we left Simon with a friend and headed out to the Special Children's Center. By Ithaca standards the drive was long – over ten miles. Alex was buckled into his car seat in the back of our new Ford Taurus. He was unconcerned.

"Where is this place, anyway?" I asked.

"Wilkins Road. It's on the other side of the lake."

"Oh."

"I'm scared. What are they going to say?"

"I don't know. I'm scared, too, but look, he clearly doesn't have any cognitive delays. Maybe nothing is wrong."

"You know that's not true. Do you think he's emotionally disturbed?"

"Of course not. Why would that be?"

"I don't know. I keep thinking about Andy's report. He's so sad, Dan."

"Well, maybe they'll be able to help." I was trying to be upbeat.

We arrived, parked in the lot, collected ourselves, and headed for the front door. The Center was a one-story brick building that resembled a small elementary school. It had a gym, an open area that doubled as a cafeteria and an auditorium, and a couple of hallways of fairly generic looking classrooms. Bulletin boards dotted the hallways, filled with photographs, flyers, and seasonal displays.

We let Alex open the door and went inside. The place was mostly empty but we heard a few faint echoes of kids playing somewhere in the building. We followed the signs to the main office.

"Hi, Mr and Mrs Mont," the receptionist said once we mentioned we were there for Alex.

"Hi. My last name is Goodman, said Nanette."

"Sorry."

"No problem."

From behind us came a familiar voice. "Hi Nanette!"

"Hi Sally. I guess we're in the right place."

Sally was the social worker who had interviewed us a few days earlier. She was a tall, thin woman in her twenties with short dark hair, who could quickly put people at ease. She and Nanette had made a strong connection in her brief visit.

"You doing OK?"

"About as good as can be expected. I'm glad you're here."

"Well, follow me and I'll introduce you to everybody."

"Are we going to be able to watch?"

"Oh, yeah. Of course."

We met the evaluation team. Andy was there as well as a psychologist and a speech therapist. Alex had been seen by their pediatrician earlier. After some brief introductions, we all headed down a long dimly lit hallway to a classroom. It was a large, open space with a wall of windows. Andy started playing with Alex on the floor while the psychologist briefly explained the tests Alex would take.

Alex's evaluation covered motor skills, speech, cognitive abilities, and even his sense of humor. One test, the absurdities subtest, was particularly striking. He was shown pictures and had to choose which one was absurd. For example, the evaluators would show him a picture of a person combing his hair with a fork. His evaluators reported that "his affect was very flat when looking at the pictures. It was impossible to 'read' from his face any clues as to his interpretation of the picture." Many children laugh when they see such absurd characterizations. Alex not only did not laugh, but had trouble identifying which pictures were absurd.

Another paragraph from the evaluation write-up strikes a very telling portrait of Alex at that age:

> One of the most positive things I [one of the evaluators] observed...was Alex's good temperament and willingness to be cooperative. Secondly, and more importantly, his keen observation skills and ability to focus attention are an advantage. He seems to be trying very hard to understand things he finds difficult and to learn ways to do things. As an example, a resource room teacher attending this evaluation when looking at affective skills, played a game where he would make a face and ask Alex to say whether it was happy or sad or angry. Alex found this very difficult, but was seen to be trying to both internally and externally, using his hands, mold his own face into the pattern presented by the teacher.

After a couple of hours of evaluations – an IQ test, a series of speech tests, a physical therapy evaluation – we were led to a room while the team of evaluators conferred. It was a comfortable room, but fairly sterile – like a dentist's office.

We sat at either end of a small couch and waited. I picked at a few loose threads in the couch. Nanette sat with her arms and legs crossed. There were no windows. I kept looking at the door. A box of tissues sat on a small, round table.

"A lot of crying must go on in this room," I said.

"Just you wait."

I honestly could not tell you if the people from the Special Children's Center returned in five minutes or in five hours. I do know, however, that my biggest fear was that they would come back with a statement like, "There is something terribly wrong with your son, but we don't know what it is. We have never seen a boy anything like him, but we'll do our best to devise some sort of program to help him out." For that reason, I was relieved – actually, relieved – when they filed in, sat down, and gently told us that they had seen children like Alex before, and he was autistic.

Nanette broke down in tears and reached for the tissues. I wanted to reach for Nanette, but she was deep in her own thoughts, cramming herself into the corner of the couch. The people from the center let us soak in the news for a few seconds.

"How do you feel?", they asked.

How did I feel? I felt relieved and scared and sad and nearly overwhelmed. I felt very small. A huge sense of responsibility came crushing down on me. I tried to pull myself together.

Why was I relieved? Because I had a diagnosis, and a diagnosis meant a plan. But I was sad, too. I was sad for Alex. What would his life be like? Autistic? I knew next to nothing about autism. Would he have friends? Would he fall in love? For Christ's sake, would he be able to live on his own and not in an institution? He was my little boy – vulnerable and sweet – and all he had to help him through the world was me and Nanette.

I was scared. My younger sister had a tough time growing up. I knew how problem children can tear a family apart, how they can destroy marriages, overwhelm lives. I knew firsthand the emotional energy that such a child entails. I had seen it rip at my own parents. What would it do to Nanette and me? What would it do to Simon?

Nanette sobbed and I wanted to comfort her, but I felt awkward. My first inclination is to want to fix things, but there was really nothing I could do at that moment. I moved closer on the couch.

"OK. You say he is autistic," said Nanette, "but now what?"

"You know your son. You know he has lots of strengths. He's smart and seems to have a strong desire to learn how to interact with people. That's going to help him a lot."

"He's the same boy he was before the diagnosis," said Sally.

Yes, I thought, but "autism" is a scary word. It conjures images of people totally shut off from the world, rocking in a corner, expressing no happiness or love. That wasn't Alex. His autism was obviously a less severe variety. Diagnosis or no diagnosis, he was unhappy and troubled.

"The fact that they diagnosed him as autistic is good, Nanno. It's better than them throwing up their hands."

"You're right but I'm still not happy about it."

"I know."

"At least there are other kids like him. We'll know where to start."

He had a diagnosis. That meant smart people had thought hard about how his mind worked and how to help him. Teachers and therapists had experience working with similar children. I was shaken but I was also empowered.

Diane never had a definitive diagnosis. She had seen a raft of specialists and received a lot of therapy but nobody was ever sure what was wrong, how she might develop. Alex's problems were more severe, and they were not things he would just outgrow. His development would not "even out" as we had been told many times, but maybe we could understand it. Hard work lay ahead of us. But we were already working hard. Now we had hope we would learn how to work smart, too.

We sat up together that night and talked and cried for hours. We berated ourselves for being dense but we reassured each other we were doing the best we knew how. We went over the material the people at the Special Children's Center gave us. The more we read, the more obvious it became that the evaluation team was right.

We called our families to give them the news.

"Mom? Hi, it's Dan."

"Did you get back from that place? What did they say? I've been sitting by the phone all day."

"They said he's autistic."

"Oh shit! Really?"

"Yeah, but it's better that way. At least now we know what we're dealing with. We can have a plan."

"I know, Daniel. You'll do the right thing. You and Nanette are smart, well-educated, wonderful parents, but...Look, I know what it feels like, OK? I'm not just thinking about Alex. I'm thinking about you. Your heart aches when something is wrong with your child."

"Yeah, I'm kind of in a whirl right now."

"Well, I know you'll do the right things, but I wish you didn't have to go through all this. How's Nanette taking the news?"

"She's upset. She's crying. We're both crying."

"Just remember, he's the same lovable little boy he was before this diagnosis. Now you'll find out how to help him."

"Yeah, that's exactly what the social worker said."

"I know what you're going through, Daniel, believe me. I wish you didn't have to. There's nothing worse than worrying about your child."

I spoke with my mother every few days after that for months. It helped that she had gone through so much with my little sister. Only people with similar problems really know how you feel. They know the tumult you go through and the uncertainty of not knowing whether you'll be up to the task. The nagging doubts. The fear that the hassles of daily life are distracting you from the job at hand.

Someone who's been there can help you laugh, too, and not feel they need to provide heavy-handed support or encouraging words. They can let you ride the waves of dismay, confusion, hope, absurdity, and relief. They can let you complain.

It's important to complain. When you say, "He's been having fits all day; I want to pull my hair out" you want to hear "Oh, brother. I know what you mean. You live for bedtime." Not, "Well, all children have bad days." When you say, "He walked up to a one-year-old and asked them to play Risk. The boy has no conception of the difference between a child and an adult" you want to hear "Are you kidding?" Not, "Well he is such a smart little boy, playing Risk at his age." When you say "He and Simon have nothing in common. Nothing. I'm running two separate activities all day long" you don't want to hear "All brothers fight."

Yes, all brothers fight. Yes, all children have tantrums. Yes, all kids have trouble sometimes figuring out the world. But we're talking magnitude here, people, and constancy. We're talking a qualitative difference.

"Look, Dan. Your friends aren't going to get it unless they've been there. Your father and I had a lot of problems with people because of Diane."

* * * * *

The one part of his evaluation that we were not totally at ease with, though, was the speech part. His speech evaluation described his echolalia and active speech (i.e. talking) but we felt it underestimated his ability to understand language.

When the speech therapist asked Alex, "How did you get here today?" Alex did not answer the question. He merely echoed back, "How did you get here today?" We knew that he was capable of answering that question. We were afraid that he was sending the wrong signal. We thought his level of understanding was much higher than his ability to form language. He also didn't identify words that we were sure that he knew. Therefore, we felt they were underestimating his ability to understand language. The first thing we did was to take him to a center in Syracuse for another evaluation.

As in the evaluation in Ithaca, Alex did not respond very well when asked to identify the meaning of words. The therapist evaluating Alex had an idea. Instead of asking him to verbally answer questions, he was allowed to type the answers – by himself, without any assistance – into a Canon Communicator, a little handheld device resembling an electric typewriter. His test scores on receptive language rose dramatically:

> Alex's highly developed reading skills and his interest in written communication may serve as the key to unlocking the door to his expressive language. The Canon Communicator allowed Alex to increase his mean length of response, answer questions and decrease echolalia. He appears to fit into the group of autistic persons whose expressive communication style is hampered by the processes involved in verbal output. In the 1990 (Vol. 4) issue of *Autism Research Review* an autistic child printed on his communicator, "I do not decide not to talk. My brain decides." Alex may well feel burdened by the same conflict.

In the end, I am not sure how much of a difference this made to Alex's speech therapy. In fact, as we later learned through working with Katie, the speech therapist at the Special Children's Center, and other speech specialists, his refusal to answer the question "How did you get here?" was the result of a speech problem. In fact, the two sets of testing results

---

*   Rimland, B. (1990) 'Suprising Success Reported with Facilitated Communication.' *Autism Research Review International* 4, 4, 1–2

were not inconsistent. Alex had a great vocabulary but he lacked the ability to figure out, from the context of the situation, exactly what was being asked. When the interviewer asked, "How did you get here today?" did she mean "What mode of transportation?" or did she mean, "Who drove the car?" or did she mean "What streets did you travel on?" Several possible interpretations existed, and overwhelmed by not knowing what was asked he just shut down.

Katie, who also did his original evaluation, devised an excellent curriculum for him. She had a good rapport with him, and by the end of the year had him actually engaging in conversations – short conversations, grant you, but he was on his way to communicating verbally in a limited but much more effective manner. Nevertheless, the experience with the Canon Communicator clued us in to the fact that often things could be going on inside his head that he wasn't able to share with us. The world is still a tough place to figure out for Alex, and he misses a lot of what is going on around him, but again and again we discover that there is more awareness and more taking place inside him than we realize.

15

"My Son, the Doctor"

☙

"The day you were born, your father cried," said my mother. "He said that he knew his purpose in life was to father a doctor."

One day I was alone with my father in an elevator. As the door closed, he said "I don't think there's anything wrong with living vicariously through your son."

"What!?" I said, flabbergasted.

"Your success is my success."

"How can you say that? Talk about pressure."

"There's nothing wrong with pressure."

All through my childhood I dutifully reported that my life's ambition was, indeed, to be a physician. Therefore, it came as something of a shock when I rebelled in college and said I would be...an economist. My parents were furious and crushed. If they were paying the bills I think they would have considered yanking some of my financial support.

"Why should we pay for fancy-shmancy Swarthmore College if you're just going to waste it by not going into medicine?"

"You're not paying. I'm going here on my own savings and my own scholarships. Besides, I didn't say I was going to be a poet! I said an economist, for God's sake. I have friends majoring in religion whose parents would give anything for an economist."

My rebellion was probably one of the puniest on record.

"What are you going to do with an economics degree?" my dad asked.

College and college majors and the world of BAs and PhDs were alien to my parents. They were bright, hardworking people but it wasn't something with which they were familiar.

They didn't want me to struggle. They thought the best way to ensure that was if I were to be a doctor. Then, I'd be my own boss and I'd have a valuable skill that would always be in demand and always well compensated (I guess they didn't foresee the rise of managed care.)

"It's important to be your own boss," said my dad. "I never want you going with your hat in your hand asking for some job. And besides, sometimes people aren't so quick to hire Jews in business."

"Are you kidding?" I said. What era was he living in, I thought. "I've never experienced any anti-Semitism in my life."

"You're only a kid."

"I'm almost 20 years old, Dad. I'm an adult."

"You think you're an adult."

In truth, what I secretly dreamed about was a career as a writer or an actor. I had acted in many shows in high school. It was my passion. It let me throw my shyness to the wind and let myself go. It let me discover things about myself and experience the thrill of being exposed and on the edge.

Those dreams were phantoms, though. I lacked the drive and guts to pursue those careers. When I mentioned them to my parents they recoiled in horror, and given all they had gone through for me (and their troubles with Diane), I just put them on the shelf.

When I went off to college, they actually forbade me to act. My freshman year I auditioned anyway and landed a lead in a production. I figured I just wouldn't tell them. I didn't want to argue and I didn't want any grief.

"Guess what?" my dad told me over the phone. "We subscribed to the Phoenix – you know, the Swarthmore newspaper."

I quickly called the editor.

"Look, when you do a story on the show, don't mention me or put my picture in the paper."

"But you're the lead."

"My parents will kill me."

"OK, but that's weird."

By the next year I just bagged the whole acting thing. I went to plays with a lump in my throat and made a couple of halfhearted attempts to write one, but theater quickly faded from my life. I left science behind completely, and majored in economics with a minor in math. When I graduated I went to the University of Wisconsin's economics graduate program on a full fellowship.

"We're so proud of you, Dan," said my mother. "I look at you and I think I must've done something right with my life."

"Will you please stop saying that?"

"So what will you do, anyway, with a PhD in economics?" asked my father.

"I don't know. Teach."

"Teach other people so they can teach other people?"

"I can do lots of things – teach, do public policy, work for a bank…"

"Well, we're really proud of what you've already accomplished," said my mom.

"That's right, Tiger. I just wanted to know exactly what it is you're going to *do*."

16

"Believe Me, They'd Have a Schedule!"

☙

I have a better understanding of autism now than when Alex was diagnosed. People fall into a broad spectrum of autistic behaviors, and although scientific studies have found that physical differences exist between the brains of people with autism and neurologically typical (NT) people, autism is still diagnosed according to a list of behaviors. If a person exhibits a certain number of these behaviors, then he or she is considered to be autistic.

The people at the Special Children's Center gave us that list. Reading that was like something out of the *Twilight Zone*. All the things that we felt were Alex's idiosyncrasies were written down in black and white. The little bundle of attributes and odd behaviors that we thought were special to Alex, were right there in front of us in a published list. It was like a bizarre Chinese restaurant menu. "Choose one from column A, and two from column B." Reading each item was akin to having a hammer beating down on top of my head. His was a classic case.

One of the nice things about Alex having a diagnosis was that right away there were things we could do. We gathered reading material and searched out parents of other autistic children. There's no friend like one who is going through the same thing as you are.

Autism is rare enough – especially cases like Alex's where the autistic person is relatively high-functioning – that it can be difficult to find parents of similar children. Ithaca is not very large, and we feared being unable to hook up with other people going through a similar ordeal.

To our surprise, Sally told us that there were actually three little boys in Ithaca similar to Alex who had been to the Special Children's Center, and she offered to contact their parents for us to see if they'd be willing to meet with us.

They were eager to do so. Finding another parent of an autistic child is like stumbling on a member of a secret club with whom you form an immediate bond.

Nanette arranged a meeting with two of the mothers and their sons, who were slightly older than Alex. They met in the backyard of one of the moms. Needless to say, the children didn't have much to do with each other, but the connections between the women were fast and furious.

Routines. Transitions. Games. Dr Seuss marathons. Learning to read effortlessly. Spinning objects. Bland food. Fear of or indifference to other children. The growing realization that something was wrong. The evaluation. The shock. The fears. The thought, "What do we do next?"

"Oh God. When you get the diagnosis it's like the floor falls out from under you."

"Tell me about it."

"I mean, autism? I thought they were nuts. He doesn't rock in the corner all day."

"My doctor said he can't be autistic because he looks at you. Shows how much he knows."

"My parents still don't believe the diagnosis, and we've been to three clinics."

"I'm tired of explaining these things."

"Yeah, I'm going to get some note cards printed up and hand them out whenever anyone says something."

"I'm just going to put a sign around my neck – 'I am not a bad mom. My child is autistic.'"

"Or how about, 'Leave my kid alone and, believe me lady, he'll leave you alone, too.'"

"Then our kids could all live in a group home and leave each other alone together!"

"But who'd get to turn off the lights?"

"Believe me, they'd have a schedule."

The women decided that all of our families should meet. I was eager to do so, more to see the other boys than meet the parents. They were a little older, after all – only a year or two, but still, it was a window into what I could expect from Alex's development. We arranged for a barbecue. There were four families in all.

The weather was delightful and the house we gathered at had an elevated deck that looked out on over an acre of land. It was a typical large, lush Ithaca backyard out in the country. The woods were alive with deer and rabbits. The yard was neatly but not overly landscaped. We sat on the deck eating burgers and drinking beer.

I didn't spend too much time taking in the scenery, though. I kept glancing at the boys. The oldest one, a third grader, actually seemed able to carry on a conversation, although he was easily agitated and somewhat argumentative. Another boy who was a year older than Alex and just starting kindergarten was less anxious. I was encouraged.

We compared notes on behavior, evaluations, and schooling options. It was a relief to hear that both of the school-aged boys were being mainstreamed. There were few private school options in Ithaca. That made us heavily reliant on the public schools.

Unfortunately I had a difficult time connecting with the other fathers. They were more reticent about exchanging stories about their children. I suspected one father was not convinced of his son's diagnosis. He thought his wife was being overly concerned and protective.

We tried meeting parents of other autistic children, but often their children were much lower functioning – non-verbal, even non-communicative. Some had serious cognitive delays and some expressed almost no emotions whatsoever. We felt guilty talking about our problems and challenges. Our fears were smaller, our problems not as overwhelming, and our relationships with our children more developed. We almost felt we had no right to gripe or be worried.

But raising a high-functioning autistic child is difficult enough, emotionally as well as merely having to confront the problems of getting through the day. One little boy we met that day later became combative and ended up in a residential home, his mother on Prozac, his parents' marriage kaput, and his siblings angry and resentful. But the other families we met at the barbecue remain strong. One mom, who Nanette keeps in regular touch with even though we now live far away – especially when the problems or joys of raising an autistic child get particularly intense – she refers to as her soul mate.

17

An Integrated Classroom

೮෪

The first thing the Special Children's Center did was send Andy to advise us on how to start teaching Alex. Andy gave us some games to play with Alex and helped us understand autism better, but the core of what he told us to do was remarkably similar to what we had already been doing. He told us that Alex needed structure and explanations. He needed the world to be interpreted for him. He needed repetition, and he needed security. But he also needed to be stretched gently, not thrown into the pool to sink or swim, but not kept wrapped in a cocoon, either. Learning that our instincts had been good was probably the most comforting thing that happened to us at that time.

An important goal, said Andy, was getting Alex to pretend. Pretend play involved paying attention to others' behavior, mimicking it, and getting inside it to make it your own. Generalizing from others' behavior is an important skill – a skill that Alex did not have. We tried to use Simon as a guide and his toys as tools.

Simon had a Playskool kitchen. It came with a little set of dishes and silverware. We also had some fake food – rubber lettuce, purple plastic grapes, yellow cheese, foam bread, and some brown disks that were supposed to be bologna.

"Here, Alex. I'm making a sandwich. Would you like a drink?"

With no emotion, Alex raised the empty cup to his lips and held his sandwich as we sat around a towel that was supposedly a picnic blanket.

Our picnics became routine and mechanical. Andy told us it was a first step. I felt silly.

When we had "picnics" with Simon, his imagination whizzed into overdrive. The little brown disks *were* bologna. His little action figures ate ten-course meals. We cleaned, cooked, ate, and poured. Simon's chatter was non-stop. The play grew organically. Where Simon reveled in pretend play, Alex tolerated our attempts with stoicism and some confusion.

"Have you played Hide and Seek?" asked Andy.

"A little."

"That's a good game because it gets Alex thinking about the world from another person's point of view. Plus it's interactive but still structured."

On one of our many trips to the toy store, we happened upon a game called Kids On Stage. The object of this game, like so many others, is to get to the finish line first. You roll a die and move along a multicolored path. While moving along this path, however, you had to play Charades. The colored squares corresponded to three categories of cards. One color stood for objects, one for actions, and another for animals. A player had to convey what was on the card they picked without using any words. This game was the only way we could get Alex to even attempt to use his imagination, both in terms of guessing what we were doing and getting him to try and pretend. Eventually he learned all the cards and had memorized particular actions for each one. In the process, however, he at least began to stretch his imagination. When we told Katie about this game, she immediately incorporated it in her speech therapy.

The experts we saw and the books we read told us that most things about the world whizzed by Alex's head in confusion. He had difficulty absorbing information from the outside world, and integrating what his senses brought into his head. He was overwhelmed. He therefore developed strategies to limit that confusion. Keeping to a strict routine was one mechanism. Another was his echolalia. Remember, his echolalia was most acute when he was being questioned. A question clearly signified that something was expected of him. Often, he didn't know what.

Repeating the question was a way of responding, seemingly in context. I mean, "What the hell, those words worked for Daddy, why not for me?" Not that the process is that conscious. Needless to say, when I learned all this I was chagrined and felt awful for all the times I lost my patience and yelled at the poor little guy. Once we knew what was going on, we viewed echolalic responses as a sign and not some inexplicable annoyance.

We realized that in whatever way we wanted to open up the world for Alex – be it the world of imagination, social mores, or social interaction – it would have to be limited by understandable boundaries.

His love and need for structure explained a lot of other things about him, too. For example, when Alex was little his favorite reading material consisted of recipes and instruction manuals. Even today he dives with glee into instructions to new games or new appliances. He gets absorbed in maps and charts. He even used to read an old book of my father's that consisted of nothing but different math tables, uncovering patterns in logarithm and trigonometry charts. He laughed while learning metric conversion.

The summer went by quickly. I was anxious, though, for school to start. Alex would be going to school at the Special Children's Center, and I was impatient for his "treatment" to begin. Everything we read stressed how important early intervention was, and I wanted the intervening to get under way full steam ahead.

I was eager to get Alex into any program at the Special Children's Center. I very much wanted him to be with professionals experienced with autistic children as soon as possible. Nanette, however, had been a little skittish about sending Alex to the Special Children's Center.

"Come on, Nanette, where else is he going to go?"

"I don't know if I want him being surrounded by kids with disabilities. After all, he has a social learning disability. How is he going to learn appropriate ways to interact if he is only with kids who don't know how to interact?"

"But a regular school isn't going to know how to deal with him."

"I'm not leaping at the first thing."

"I don't want to wait around. I want to do something."

"Well, let's see what they say, but they're going to have to convince me."

She was right. Was I looking for the easy way out, or was I just being impatient? Then again, what were the alternatives? I wanted to do something *now*. I didn't want more time to slip away.

We went back to the Special Children's Center. They suggested an integrated classroom. As we learned what they meant, I sighed with relief. That meant Alex's class would be evenly split between typical children without any kind of developmental problem and children with a variety of disabilities, but many functioning above Alex's level.

The integrated classroom satisfied both our concerns. Thankfully, Nanette and I usually see eye to eye. It is unsettling on the rare occasions when we don't. We both want the world for Alex and know our decisions about parenting him are very important and usually not clear-cut. To not feel like we are part of a team would be wrenching.

In the end, we both agreed that exposing Alex to typical children should be an important part of his education. Unpredictability flusters Alex. Children with special needs are often unpredictable. At the time, Alex did not know how to approach children, talk to them, or deal with them in any constructive way. His speech was not normal. We couldn't envision him in a regular classroom. On the other hand, a self-contained, special needs classroom has never seemed the appropriate setting for him because even though Alex has profound problems, he functions at a higher level than many children with special needs do. In many academic disciplines, he surpasses the vast majority of children. And when he is bored, his bad behaviors become more severe.

The integrated classroom seemed to offer the best of both worlds. The student–teacher ratio was very low. The staff was trained to deal with children with special needs and had lots of experience. And lastly, half of Alex's classmates would be typical children whom he could get used to and learn from.

This last point turned out to be not quite as true as we had originally hoped. Painfully, we have discovered that Alex doesn't learn well from role models. He does not generalize from social situations or make inferences about the rules of social behavior like other children do.

Nevertheless, being in a class with typical children has always contributed very positively to Alex's education. First because they are more predictable and explicable, but another advantage is that since typical children view Alex as a person with a disability, they have often been protective of him and generous when it comes to helping him. Our fears of him being picked on, teased, or bullied never really materialized throughout his time in nursery or elementary school.

Who would send their typical children to an integrated program? Who were these children? If I did not have a child with special needs, I am not sure I would have done so at the time. It turns out that many of Alex's classmates were the children of staff at the center. Not only was the school convenient and excellent, but more importantly, I would like to believe the staff thought their typical children could learn from children with special needs. Children can develop a deeper understanding that people have weaknesses as well as strengths. Sometimes the strengths are hidden but that doesn't mean they are less profound. And I think children can come to appreciate their own abilities and find the nurturer within themselves.

18

Crazy, Incomprehensible Rules

CЗ

Alex's school day started with an hour-long bus ride. A little yellow school bus would back into our driveway at 7:20, and Nanette would run out with Alex. The bus driver, a heavy-set gregarious woman would strap Alex in his seat, and the bus would head out to the next stop. A few children were already on the bus at this point, one in a specialized wheel chair.

After picking up a few more children in town, the bus would head to the other side of Lake Cayuga, the long, deep lake that runs along one side of town, and up a hill to the Special Children's Center.

Alex was met at the bus by his teacher or an aide. The first challenge was negotiating the doorway. Alex wanted to open the door, but this was not allowed. Too many children were constantly passing through it. He would have a fit. Over a shorter time than we imagined – a couple of months – he was firmly but gently broken of this habit. The key, though, was that he wasn't treated like an obstinate, intractable little brat, but an autistic boy who longed for routine but needed to learn flexibility. He was not punished or reprimanded, but firmly explained the rules and forced to live with them.

Early in the school year Nanette sometimes drove Alex to school herself. We both felt bad that a boy not quite four years old had to sit on a bus ride that long that early in the morning. He'd talk to no one but just sit staring out the window. Nanette could get Alex to school in 15 minutes, drop by Dunkin' Donuts with Simon on the way home, and still have a full day ahead of her.

Once in the school building, Alex walked down a long hallway to his classroom. He was met by about 12 other students, his teacher, an aide, and often Katie or another therapist, or possibly a social worker. His teacher, Amy, was young and energetic. She had short, curly blonde hair, long limbs, and a toothy smile. She took a quick liking to Alex, and had a level of patience with him that had long since abandoned us.

Amy's class was tailor-made for Alex. Circle time, for instance, which had been the bane of his existence, became effortless. Why? Because the circle in his new classroom was clearly delineated by a set of stars painted on the floor. When circle time rolled around, his teacher, Amy, would simply announce that everyone should go sit on a star. Alex thought this was fun. Having a visual representation of the circle and knowing exactly where to go and what to do was very relaxing. He could focus on the narrow task of finding a star, sitting on it, and staying on it. The fact that such a minor innovation could make such a large impact on Alex's life was amazing.

Day after day, Alex's teachers coaxed him to come out of his shell and engage the world. They worked on approaching other children with requests, taking turns, and simply being comfortable with another person in your "space."

The room was divided up into different stations – a water table or a drawing table, for example – and a limit of three children would be allowed at each station. Amy or Katie would make sure that any time interaction was called for – maybe Alex wanted something being used by another child – Alex spoke to that child and attempted to make eye contact.

Alex's days varied.

"Nanette, can you stick around for a minute. I'd like to talk to you about something," said Amy.

"Sure."

"You know how you drop Alex off sometimes?"

"Yes. That bus ride is ridiculously long."

"Well, actually, Alex seems to have a better day when you *don't* drive him."

"Really?"

"Yes, I think the bus ride gives him some transition time. By time he gets here he's in school mode."

"So you're saying, 'Back off Mom!'"

"Well," Amy laughed, "kind of."

One major goal for Alex was that by the end of the year he learned how to take part in conversations. Alex did not have real conversations. He would parrot back what was said to him. He would make a request, or even answer a direct question if it was clear enough. However, he never engaged in the give and take of a real conversation. He wouldn't carry the thread of a topic, give his opinion about something, or comment on what you said in response to something he had said. He used speech for very utilitarian purposes.

The first step to building conversational skills with Alex was to get him to participate in an exchange of three related sentences. Katie, his speech therapist, or Amy would say one sentence; Alex would be asked to respond with a related sentence, and Katie and Amy would then contribute a third sentence, with Alex focusing on what they were saying. Then, they would write these down on paper and review them. A more advanced conversation would begin with Alex offering the first sentence. This accomplishment took months of painstaking effort.

Conflict resolution and getting along with others were other major subject areas. Of course, these are major parts of any pre-school curriculum. A normal pre-school setting, however, would not have been as effective. A regular pre-school teacher would not have the skills or resources to construct rules with unflagging consistency, break them down into digestible components, and spoon feed them. A regular schoolteacher wouldn't have the extra classroom staff or the specialists to pull in for one-on-one or small group sessions. Most importantly, a regular schoolteacher would have been less likely to appreciate how Alex learned.

Sometimes when Alex gets fixated on or disturbed about something, he needs to have an explanation to put him at ease. A response of,

"Because that's the way it is" or "Because I said so" can cause a fit. Occasions arise when for a typical child that is an appropriate response. The answer is too complicated or there isn't enough time to go into details. Children sometimes just need to have rules laid out for them, even if they appear arbitrary. The older a child gets, of course, the more explanations he or she deserves.

Responses like "That's just the way it has to be right now," however, are like pouring gasoline on hot coals when it comes to Alex. First of all they make no sense to his highly logical mind. Secondly, they don't alleviate the fear and internal tumult that arises when the world does not make sense.

"Well," he thinks, "If that inexplicable thing has to be, then what other crazy incomprehensible rules are people going to throw at me?"

One of the best examples of the kind of teaching that Alex needs – and each plea for an explanation is a signal that "here is a teachable moment" – comes from an experience in Alex's first grade class.

Alex was mainstreamed in a regular first-grade classroom. His teacher had told the class that if she asked a question, children who had the answer should raise their hands and wait to be called upon. This rule made sense to Alex and he obeyed. Alex generally had all the answers to math-related questions and his hand always shot up in the air. He often rose to his feet and waved his hand almost bursting from trying to hold in the answer.

Sometimes, contrary to her stated policy, the teacher called on children who did not have their hand raised. Alex would burst into tears. He would scream. He would shout, "He did not have his hand raised!" He would roll on the floor. Needless to say, this disruption could not be tolerated. Disciplining him, however, did not work.

At night, when I would ask Alex about this situation, he would instantly become teary eyed. He would get sad and angry and he would berate the teacher for calling on someone whose hand was not raised. A rule had been explained to him, and rules were something you were supposed to be able to rely on, especially a rule that made sense to him, like the hand-raising rule.

"Alex," I said, "do you know the reason for the rule that children have to raise their hands?"

"So the teacher knows who has the answer."

"That's part of it, but there is more. Your teacher has to make sure that everyone is paying attention and learning what she is trying to teach. If she sees that some kids are not ever raising their hands, she has to find out if they are just shy or if they are not listening or if they don't know the answers. If that's the case, then she has to work harder to teach them better. The rule of raising your hand is for helping her know what is going on in the class."

Once Alex absorbed this reasoning his tantrums over hand-raising stopped overnight. Literally. The world made sense. We used to say that as long as Alex could be continually accompanied by a social interpreter he would be OK. His pre-school class at the Special Children's Center always had an interpreter nearby.

One thing he needed help interpreting was facial expressions. Alex could not tell if someone was happy or sad or angry by the look on his or her face. His teachers used flash cards to help him learn that a smile was a sign of happiness, and that a frown meant someone was sad. More complicated or subtle expressions, though, still remain a mystery, as does most body language.

He began learning rules for interacting with people in public settings. A major field trip to McDonald's was planned for the end of the semester. The class spent a few weeks rehearsing ordering. They learned the roles of McDonald's employees and were familiarized with the menu. They practiced speaking to people. I'm not certain about this, but my guess is they talked about who would open the door.

They tried to teach him to pretend, but that proved more difficult. Unlocking Alex's imagination has proven a tough lock to pick. When we offered him pretend games he gave us a blank stare, like we were nuts. Most small children love to pretend. Half of Simon's life was pretend. His little plastic animals and action figures came to life. Cops and Robbers. Cowboys and Indians. Pretending is one of the main things kids do. Nanette sewed little costumes for him – Peter Pan, Captain Hook, King Arthur – and he'd play in his imaginary world for hours. And Nanette would join him. She sewed a Peter Pan outfit for herself, too. That's one of the joys of having a small child – being allowed to re-enter that pretend world for yourself.

Not until I began watching Simon grow up did I truly come to understand how unusual Alex was with his lack of imaginative play. I obtained a little insight into Alex's world when he was about five years old and Simon was three. We had just come from a performance of "Peter and the Wolf." Alex generally hated movies, videos, TV shows, or any kind of performance. This was a children's ballet, however, and he seemed to enjoy it somewhat, or at least tolerate it.

As soon as we arrived home, Simon said he wanted to play "Peter and the Wolf." "Great," I thought, "I just explained the story to Simon and Alex at the theater. Alex should have some structure to build on in re-enacting the tale." By this time Alex was diagnosed and we were told to try and engage him in imaginative play. This was a golden opportunity.

"Let's play Peter and the Wolf," said Simon.

"Great idea. Alex, do you want to play Peter and the Wolf with us?"

"How do you play?"

"You see," said Simon, "you just do the story."

"What do you mean, 'Do the story'?"

"Alex. It's like this," I explained. "We each pretend we are a character in the story, and we do all the things we saw them do in the show."

"How do you know when it ends?"

"When we have a parade with the wolf all tied up. That's the last thing that happens in the story."

"That game is too difficult. I don't want to play."

Difficult. He didn't say "boring" or "stupid," but difficult. That moment was an epiphany for me. It was then that I began to fully appreciate what I intellectually knew from reading. For Alex, all social interactions would have to be decomposed into a set of rules – into scripts of behavior to be learned, memorized, and then internalized.

Alex lives by the rules, by the structure. There are rules to playing a "game" like "Peter and the Wolf", and a very fluid structure, but they were opaque to Alex. The rules to a pretend game are arguably more complex than a game like Monopoly. It's just that most of us are hard-wired to absorb them. At age five, this child could play Monopoly, Risk, Stratego, and any number of well-structured games. He could not, however, handle the difficulties involved with "Peter and the Wolf."

In fact, we had major altercations when Alex and Simon were five-and three years old because of Alex's inability to distinguish pretending from lying.

"Zoom. I'm going up to the moon."

"Simon is lying!!! He is NOT going to the moon."

"I know he isn't going to the moon, Alex, but..."

"Yes I am! This is a spaceship and I'm going up to the moon."

"He is lying!" cried Alex as he burst into tears. "Lying is bad!"

"He isn't lying. He is pretending."

"What's the difference?"

"Pretending is when you are having fun making believe something is true when everyone knows that it isn't."

"How do you KNOW that everyone knows it isn't true?"

"Well, because it is very clear that we are not in a spaceship."

"How do I know that Simon knows that?"

"Because this is a car, and Simon knows what a car is. The point is that when you pretend you aren't trying to fool a person into believing something that isn't true. You are just going along for the fun of pretending something."

"It's FUN to LIE?"

"It's not lying. It is pretending."

And Simon says, "And I'm going to fight some moon men."

"There are NO MEN ON THE MOON!"

Tears. Screams. You can't tell a three-year-old to stop pretending. That's like telling him not to eat or breathe. Besides, it isn't fair. And of course, this was one of those proverbial "teachable moments." Anyway, several weeks of belabored explanations and answering every loophole in every characterization of the difference between lying and pretending that Alex would unerringly discover, got us past that problem.

Imagine, though, the task of having to learn concepts such as these step by step – of having to convert the intuitive into the analytical. The thought exhausts me. The task boggles my mind.

19

Exhausted

❧

"Exhausted" is the word that most invokes those times for me. Nanette and I were often strained to our limits. Some times we were anxious. Some times we were enthralled. But we were always exhausted. On top of all the diaper changing and normal running around after children, we were incessantly dealing with Alex's difficulty with others and the isolation that could bring, as well as his endless need for explanations and his being just plain intractable.

Few of our friends and family understood. "All children ask 'why' questions," they'd say. We tried to explain that Alex's questions were more frequent and intense. He required well-thought-out, tricky, rock-solid explanations.

"All children need care and constant supervision."

Yes, but Alex – who was getting to the age where this generally eased up – needed constant engagement. Hours were filled with board games and structured art projects. Hours were filled with tears and living on the edge of an anxiety attack. Plus there was Simon, who is two years younger than Alex. Sometimes with siblings there are economies of scale. The children can entertain each other – even for 15 minutes. Such was not the case with our sons. For the most part, their interests were diametrically opposed. Simon could not play board games, naturally, and Alex had zero interest in pretend play or blocks.

When taking care of both children simultaneously, we had to be running two concurrent activities. It was as if we were raising two only children in the same house.

When Nanette was home by herself she felt constantly torn in two. She remembers hour after hour of playing board games with Alex, while baby Simon was attached at her breast, nursing. It was the only way to appease both of them at the same time.

Playgroups and outings were not exactly a refuge, but they were more manageable than staying at home. As I've described earlier, Alex generally would not allow Nanette much time to interact with the other moms. Restaurants or walks along the Commons generated as much work as they did relief, but if she kept moving it was easier to keep them both engaged. Outings and activities filled her days. She was on a tread-mill perched above quicksand – stop moving and she'd get thrown off and begin to sink.

Nanette's patience and energy with Alex and Simon were super-human. But they were predicated on the belief that I would be home from work at 5:30 sharp. I would arrive home, and Nanette would sigh with relief knowing that she was ratcheted down to stand-by duty.

Sometimes I would be late. As each minute clicked past 5:30 her composure would unravel.

"Where *were* you?"

"What do you mean? It's only a quarter to six."

"You're supposed to be home at 5:30!"

"I was talking to a graduate student in the hallway and lost track of time."

"So you were just chatting in the halls when I'm dealing with these two and trying to cook dinner!"

"I'm sorry. I lost track of the time. It's only 15 minutes, for God's sake."

"Twenty. Look, I can hold it together because I know you'll be here at 5:30, not 5:45 or 6:00. I psyche myself up. At least have the decency to call me if you're going to be late. I need to know you are on your way or I can't take it."

She was right. I only had to be with Alex and Simon for a few days straight to know exactly how she felt.

One time, on a trip to Albany when I was researching New York State foster care records, I received an urgent phone call from Nanette.

"I'm sorry, Dan, but I can't take it. If you don't come home soon I'm going to lose my mind. Alex is screaming and Simon won't leave me alone for one minute. One more day of this and I'm going to shoot myself."

"Can't you put them to sleep?" I didn't want to come home.

"They won't go to sleep. And so what if they do? They'll only wake up, and I've got another whole day of this with no help. I'm so keyed up I keep screaming at them and that only makes things worse. I'm sorry. I know you're working, but I don't know what I'm going to do. I haven't had a second to myself for days."

"I'll drive back tonight."

"You're sure it's OK? Did you get enough done? I'm sorry, but..."

"Don't be sorry. For crying out loud, if I were in your place I would've beaten my head in with a baseball bat by now."

Before Alex was born, Nanette and I decided we would never hit our children, and we never have. I have to admit that we also didn't realize how strong the temptation to break our promise would be. When we were at the end of our tether, the urge to whack Alex or Simon could be pretty strong. I can understand how a single parent – especially one with other stresses in their lives – can end up abusing their child, especially a problem child. And the fact that I can understand it is a little scary.

When we were overloaded we wanted nothing more than to plop Alex down in front of the television. We just wanted a respite, a chance to breathe. Soon the thought of using the TV as a babysitter did not seem as morally reprehensible as before we were parents. Still, its seductiveness was unsettling. As much as we wanted to use the television as a source of relief we didn't want to fall into the trap of it being an easy way out that in the long run would be bad for Alex. We debated this for awhile and decided to take the Sesame Street plunge.

We checked the listings to see when the show aired, and put Alex, age three, down on the couch to watch. He looked at the screen for a few seconds and then started screaming and crying. The show was overwhelming – a sensory bombardment. Other slower-paced shows and cartoons did not freak him out, but we quickly realized that television would not be the babysitter we longed for. It was back to board games and math lessons and lengthy explanations.

Alex generally cannot handle much sensory stimulation. When he was a pre-schooler this inability to deal with a busy environment was particularly striking, though it has improved over time. Even when it comes to food, Alex likes things simple. His diet is limited and bland. Spaghetti with no sauce is a big favorite. Anything aromatic he finds repugnant. He doesn't like spicy food, food with much color, or even food with an interesting texture. When given a new food he carefully sniffs it, touches it with his fingers, and then very gingerly takes a microscopic bite. Occasionally he announces that he likes it and his limited repertoire is expanded, but usually he recoils in disgust.

Going out to a restaurant with Alex was often an adventure. Finding an acceptable menu other than one with spaghetti was a major challenge. Even fast food restaurants were a pain because of Alex's particular demands.

"May I help you?"

"Yes. I'd like a Whopper, a kid's hamburger happy meal, a chicken sandwich, two orders of fries and one more thing. A plain cheese sandwich."

"Just cheese?"

"Yes."

"Let me check on that. Meg, how do I ring up a plain cheese sandwich?" She waits for an answer. "OK, I'll have to ring that up as a cheeseburger."

"Fine. But there's just one more thing. Can you make sure the cheese is not melted and the bread is not toasted? Just cold cheese on cold bread."

"Don't toast the bread?"

"Right. Just cold cheese on cold bread. My son won't eat it if the cheese is warm."

The food comes.

"I'm sorry, but I asked you to make sure the bread was cold. You toasted the bread and the cheese melted. And you only put on one slice of cheese."

"I have to ring you up for a cheeseburger but hold the burger. That's one slice of cheese."

You've got to be kidding, I thought. But it wasn't worth the fight. I just wanted a cold cheese sandwich. "OK, but could you just put a slice of cheese on a bun but not melt the cheese?"

"You mean, not even toast the bread?"

I do not understand why this was so difficult. Drive-through windows were worse. Whenever servers got the order right on the first try I wanted to climb over the counter and kiss them.

"We'd like spaghetti with no sauce."

"No sauce? How about a little butter?"

"No. No butter. Just spaghetti."

"Plain spaghetti? "

"You got it."

The spaghetti comes and Alex cries.

"What's wrong, Alex?"

"Look at this," says Nanette. "They sprinkled oregano or something on it."

"Can you tell me what is so difficult about plain spaghetti? Waiter!"

When we did find something that Alex took to with ease, we latched on to it like a life raft, both for our sakes and also for Alex's. It was a joy to see him relaxed. It was a bigger joy to eat out in peace.

The search for peace lead to our breaking a few more promises from our pre-parent days. One of which was buying a Nintendo game system.

Alex was four years old when we bought Nintendo and he took to it like a fish takes to water. We attached the system to the television in our room. Our TV sat on the corner of Nanette's dresser near the foot of our bed. It was a small 12-inch set, usually used to watch Johnny Carson as we fell asleep. Alex would jump up and down on the bed, his fingers busily tapping the buttons on the control pad, his eyes fixed on the screen. Sometimes he'd land on his rear end and bounce back up to his feet. I didn't understand how he could stay so focussed and be so bouncy all at the same time. His scores, though, rose steadily. He was a Nintendo whiz kid.

We didn't feel too bad because the way Alex played it was an aerobic exercise. He would laugh and squeal, totally entranced. We limited his time in front of the screen but it was a welcome relief to have a way to keep him occupied so we could do something else.

We played the Nintendo games, too. As he got older we could even talk about what we were doing. His first game was the Mario Brothers game that comes with the system. He would advance level after level, as he made Mario and Luigi bounce on top of evil mushrooms, leap across chasms, hop over fireballs and duck various hazards. The game was very structured, the scoring system made sense, the little men responded to the controls in exactly the same manner all the time, and they were always willing to play. It was heaven.

Another game we bought for Alex was called Solstice. In this game, the player controlled a little wizard character as he made his way through a huge dungeon. In each room of this dungeon there were obstacles. Some were puzzles that required logical thinking. Others required timing and good hand–eye coordination. Along the way the little wizard collected various pieces of a scepter that when completed could be used to save a princess.

One day in the backyard I noticed Alex trying to stand on a ball. He wasn't being very successful but he kept going at it.

"Dan, do you know what I think he is doing?"

"What, Nanno?"

"He's trying to balance on the ball like that little Nintendo guy. You know, the one in the Solstice game."

"My God, you're right! I've noticed he was climbing around on the playground more. I can't believe this. He's actually pretending to be the little Solstice guy."

We were very excited. Not only was Nintendo, of all things, making him more active, but maybe it was actually stimulating his imagination!

We told his teachers at the Special Children's Center about it, very pleased and less guilty about having bought the Nintendo system in the first place. Unfortunately, they told us that he really wasn't pretending. He was mimicking. He wasn't creating an imaginary world in his head and improvising. Rather he was copying something he saw. This was a more primitive type of pretending than typical children undertake. Still, it made him interact with his world a little more, and we would take that any way we could get it.

20

On the Town

❧

Nintendo or no Nintendo, we were often bursting to get out of the house. In the summer we hiked along the gorges and had picnics by the waterfalls. We also went on field trips. We'd drive down to Binghamton to go to Chucky Cheese and the Discovery Center or up to Syracuse to the zoo or to Carousel Mall. In the winter our trips were limited to area malls, the supermarket, and the occasional event, like a model train show. Ithaca had one single-level mall that we soon knew intimately.

The mall was like an interactive museum for Alex. He loved going to Kay-Bee to look at toys, Waldenbooks, or to gadget shops like Radio Shack. He loved reading signs and seeing what was on sale. The only problem was we needed eyes in the back of our head.

"Nanette, where did Alex go?"

"He was right behind me a second ago."

"Man, he disappears fast. Why can't he stay near us?"

"Because he is four. He's over there, looking at the calculators."

"No, it's more than that. He separates from us in an instant. He doesn't have any sense of where we are. Look at those other families walking through the mall. It's as if there is a big lasso around them. They kind of hang together."

"You could walk away from Alex and he could take hours for him to notice you're not there."

I tried it. Actually, what I did was let Alex wander off and I trailed behind him by about twenty feet. I felt like an actor in a bad spy thriller, trying to be unobtrusive while at the same time intent on not losing sight of him. Alex traveled the length of the mall, never aware that I was gone and never turning around to look for me. It was scary.

Generally, we preferred going to the supermarket. We spent hours every week at Wegman's, the local supermarket. It was a large, clean, airy store with a small restaurant and a large produce section. We would see shoppers come and go while we slowly made our way through the store, with Alex safely in one grocery cart and Simon in the other. When Alex got a little big for the seat, he would ride in the back of one cart with Simon in the front while we pushed another cart laden with groceries. If Nanette or I went to the store by ourselves, we would have to maneuver two carts through the aisles, one loaded with children, the other with food. Sometimes Nanette would actually nurse Simon while she maneuvered the carts. Nanette said that feat impressed her own mother more than anything else she has ever done.

Alex absolutely adored Wegman's. It was the highlight of his week. He fired off questions in rapid succession, hungry for answers.

"Why is the unit price smaller for the 128 ounce size than the 64 ounce size?"

I had to explain about volume discounts – not just that they existed but the reasoning behind them. Simple explanations would not suffice. Our discussions became very involved.

"You see Alex there are fixed costs and variable costs. The cost of advertising for the product and shipping it doesn't depend on the volume, but the cost of the detergent does."

"Why do they put things on sale?"

"To sell more."

"But that doesn't mean the people spend more money."

"That's right, Alex. It depends on the price elasticity of demand. If the quantity sold increases by a greater percentage than the price of the good was decreased, the good is called elastic. Then, lowering the price will increase revenue."

Eventually we started talking about loss leaders and brand loyalty. I got the strangest looks from other shoppers. One moment I was trying to explain to Alex the difference between a horse and a dog – he didn't know. The next minute I was giving him an economics lecture. Then I'd be dealing with his screaming because another child said hello to him. Then, he'd be rattling off unit prices or ratios he figured out in his head.

But it was fun. Alex came alive in the supermarket. He talked more there than anywhere else. When he was about five years old it was one of our main opportunities to actually converse. And his ability to absorb information and apply math to the world around him was awesome. Alex has always loved and been intrigued by math and anything resembling a system. He could be entertained indefinitely with these discussions.

With Alex safely contained in the grocery cart, I could concentrate on either Alex or shopping but I never had to feel like I had eyes in the back of my head. Nanette and I would slowly stroll the aisles and talk. In a mall, we were constantly on our guard. We could not turn our gaze from Alex for 15 seconds without him wandering off, or if we were the ones doing the walking, without him being left behind.

One day, Nanette took the boys to the mall while I was at work. It was a common outing on bad weather days. Nanette was looking at a display of sandals. Simon was in the stroller and Alex was at her side checking out the prices. Nanette turned to go, but didn't see Alex.

"Alex?...Alex!"

She spun around but he was nowhere to be seen. Her heart sank to her stomach. This is every parent's nightmare, when a minute feels like an hour. This child could not recognize a soul. He could also be terrified by anyone approaching him. On the other hand, if he was engaged in something he thought was interesting, he could be oblivious for hours to the fact that he was alone.

"I can't find my little boy," she said hurriedly, running up to a security guard.

"What does he look like?"

"He's five years old and he has blonde hair. He's dressed...wait a minute...oh, yeah, he's dressed in blue shorts and a gray shirt."

"Don't worry, ma'am. We'll find him."

Mall security went into their lost child drill. Security guards ran to each mall exit and then started walking towards the center of the mall, scanning every store. No announcement was made over the loud-speaker. Nanette asked why.

"It's not a smart idea to publicize to a mall full of people that there is a little boy ripe for the picking."

Good point.

They found him after awhile. He was unfazed. Nanette wasn't. We became neurotic about keeping him in sight until he was about in fifth grade. By then, he seemed to have some sense of staying with us. In fact, if he loses sight of us he almost goes into a panic now. It's as if his behavior in this regard is like a child of much younger years.

I was lost as a child once. My family had driven from Jersey to Coney Island in Brooklyn for the day to go to the beach. We lived in Elizabeth at the time. I was three years old.

"Daddy, I want to get some water for my castle."

"OK, I'll help you."

"I wanna do it myself."

"All right, but go straight down to the water and come straight back." We were less than ten yards from the shoreline. I was annoyed. Did they think I was a baby? I took my pail to the ocean, filled it and headed back. But I thought I'd show them I was grown up. I'd circle around them.

Somehow I headed off in the wrong direction. After walking ten or fifteen minutes I knew I was lost. I kept walking and started crying. An obese woman in a flowered bathing suit, sitting in a lawn chair, called me over.

"Little boy, are you lost?"

By this time I was in tears. I could only nod.

"You better go up to the boardwalk and find a policeman."

Of course, I thought, what a dummy! They had taught me that in nursery school. I trudged up to the boardwalk and by some miracle was found by a police officer about two miles down the beach from my parents. My parents, naturally, were in a panic. The lifeguards were searching the water and my sister was crying. My father decided to take one last walk up and down the beach. I sat on a bench next to the police officer, holding his gun.

"This is heavy! Will it go off?"

"No. You can't shoot it. So tell me Danny, do you know where you live?"

"126 Berwick Street."

"Great! In what city?"

"I don't know. 126 Berwick Street."

It turns out that there is a Berwick Street in Brooklyn. They were about to take me there – about four hours after I was lost – when I spotted my dad with a huge smile on his face walking towards me. I remember being angry that my family didn't save me a Coke.

Every aspect of that long afternoon is burned in my memory. The officer's olive complexion and jet black hair, the large woman's double chin, the yellow pail I carried with me that was decorated with raised seashells, and how my fear evaporated when I spotted that cop.

Nanette and my boys have heard that story many times. Too many times.

"So Simon," I say while I'm walking in downtown DC with him and Alex. "If you got separated from me right now what would you do? And how about you, Alex?" The boys were eight and ten at the time.

"Well," said Simon after thinking a bit, "I would go into a restaurant and ask the waiter if I could call the police."

"That's a good strategy. Alex, what would you do?"

"I would find a map."

"A map? Where around here would you find a map?"

"I don't know."

"And we're 25 miles from home. How would you get there?"

"I don't know!"

Practical skills have never been Alex's strong point.

★★★★★

Needless to say, we did not go out by ourselves often when Alex was young. Your average babysitter could not handle both our sons. The screaming would be relentless and we could not enjoy ourselves knowing that Alex was anxious or miserable at home. Of course, at home we rarely had a chance to speak about anything but the kids.

"Hi Nanno. I'm home."

"Could you set the table?"

"Yeah, just let me change out of my biking clothes."

"You won't believe the day I had. We were downtown – "

"Wait a second! I have to change."

We all sat down for dinner. We always took the same chairs, Nanette and I on opposite ends with the boys across from each other. Nanette dished out the tortellini and we started eating. Simon's face was quickly covered with sauce. Alex picked up his tortellini with his fingers and crumbled it before putting it in his mouth.

"Use your fork, Alex."

"I'm using *my* fork," piped in Simon.

"Yes you are, Simon. Good job!" I said.

"So I was telling you," started Nanette.

She unleashed the torrent of her day in between wiping off the kids' faces and answering their interjections. She told me the funny stories, the exasperating moments, and her various concerns – mundane and profound. She was hungry for adult contact.

Sometimes I made the effort to talk about my day but I didn't have the energy. When I came home I generally wanted to leave that stuff behind. Then, after hearing Nanette and playing with the kids, I just wanted to watch TV or go to sleep.

"Could you pass the garlic bread?"

She passed me the bread and continued. "So Hannah –"

"Who's Hannah?"

"Hannah is Ellen's daughter."

"Ellen? She's the one with the Down's Syndrome kid, right?"

"No. That's Charla. Her daughter is Hillary."

"I can't keep them straight."

"Are you listening?"

"Yes. It's just…you can't keep the people I work with straight."

"I talk about these people all the time."

"I know, but I haven't met them. Until you meet people, it's hard to keep them straight. Speaking of which, there's a reception up at Cornell where spouses are invited."

"Oh great," she said sarcastically.

"Why? What's wrong? I thought you were starved for adult conversation."

"I hate those Cornell things."

"Why?"

"I feel so inadequate."

"What are you talking about?"

"What I'm talking about is that all those people are so smart and successful."

"You're smart."

"I'm brain dead, Dan. I only talk to children all day."

"So here's a chance to talk to adults."

"Oh great. Yes. They are all Cornell professors doing research and writing books. They ask me what I'm doing and I say I'm a stay-at-home mom, and then I get all these blank looks like, well, I guess we have nothing to talk about."

"You don't have to talk about kids. You can talk about something else."

"You don't get it. I don't have time to read the paper, let alone anything else. I play with Simon and Alex all day. I can feel myself losing IQ points."

"You're too hard on yourself. You're smart. You're an interesting person."

"The woman professors make me feel like I'm a traitor to my gender."

"They don't feel that way."

"How do you know? Anyway, I feel judged."

"If you don't want to go – "

"I'll go. I'm just telling you I have to psyche myself up. And who are we going to get to watch the kids?"

"I don't know. I can ask one of my students, I suppose."

We didn't trust high school kids. Luckily we had a supply of college and graduate students, but even still we almost never went out. The boys went to bed at about 9:00 or 10:00 and we followed soon after.

Somebody at work would ask me if I'd seen a recently released movie.

"No. Are you kidding? We never go out by ourselves."

"When was the last time you guys saw a movie?'

"I don't know. About ten months ago, I guess, when we were visiting Nanette's parents down in Florida."

"When did you have a meal, just the two of you?"

"About ten months ago, when we were visiting Nanette's parents in Florida," I repeated. "We've never been away from the kids for one night together. I go on business trips but Nanette hasn't been away from them since they day they were born."

"You guys need to get out."

The folks at the Special Children's Center asked us the same questions. Soon after they hooked us up with a respite service. Our respite worker, Ted, was in his middle thirties and had a full-time job working with mentally impaired adults. Finally, we could get out and have time to ourselves, confident that Alex and Simon were well cared for and not completely overwhelming their babysitter. The best thing about Ted was that if we went a couple of weeks without going "on a date" he would call and tell us we needed a night off. It was a blessed relief.

"Say, Nanno, want to make out in the car?"

"What?"

"It's like we're on a date, you know?"

"I don't think so. Let's go inside. We held hands walking around the Commons; that's gushy enough."

"Gushy, huh?"

"Besides it's really uncomfortable in a car. Let's go inside."

21

"That's Just Backwards Multiplication!"

⚬₰

As slow as Alex is in learning social skills, that's how quick he is when it comes to learning math or any analytical subject. The things most people learn with ease – like interpreting facial expressions, recognizing faces, generating original speech, interacting with people – Alex needs to struggle with. The things most people struggle with, however – like math, reading, science, and economics – Alex learns without effort. Actually that is an understatement. He absorbs these subjects. They enthrall and entertain him. His appetite for them is at times insatiable.

Alex's genius for math dawned on me slowly but then quickly blew me away. At age two, I was counting with him – not just by ones but by twos and threes. He learned to count so fast I can barely remember him learning at all. He seemed comfortable with counting so I explained addition to him – once – and he knew. Subtraction took another fifteen seconds. The concepts clicked in his head. Seemingly without effort he started solving for unknowns in an equation.

I would write down an equation like

$$4 + \underline{\hphantom{XX}} = 9$$

and he would immediately know that he needed to subtract four from nine to complete the equation. No explanation was necessary.

Exactly what ages he learned various math concepts I am sometimes hazy on, but before he entered kindergarten he was comfortable with all four arithmetic operations, fractions and decimals, exponents and logarithms.

"Daddy, Daddy, what is division?"

He had seen the word on a math game we had bought. At this time he already knew about multiplication.

"Alex, I don't have a lot of time right now to go into this, but...well, for example eight divided by two equals four because it takes four twos to make eight."

"Oh. That's just backwards multiplication."

End of lesson. Alex now knew how to divide. He was in pre-school.

One Saturday morning, Alex was watching General Equivalence Diploma (GED) math. Alex hated TV generally but made an exception for GED math, which I discovered early one morning while exercising. I subsequently leapt at the chance to have something Alex would sit still and do on his own for half an hour.

A question came up on the screen. Which is bigger: one-fourth or one-fifth? We had barely discussed fractions.

"One-fourth," said Alex immediately.

"How did you know that?"

"Because it takes five fifths to make one, but only four fourths."

This is a non-trivial concept, and Alex was a pre-schooler who basically figured this out on his own with no effort. Soon we were adding and subtracting fractions and then converting them to decimals.

Alex's appetite for math was insatiable. We would spend hours each day doing math. Alex would always be pushing me to learn new concepts. They delighted him. In fact, many times when we realized he had been in a bad mood for a few days we would recall that we hadn't taught him anything new in math recently. I would sit down and show him something new, like exponents or probability, and he would immediately perk up.

When he was crying or particularly unnerved we would pose math problems for him to solve. They were more effective and fast acting than any tranquilizer. Long car trips often felt like math marathons.

He wasn't even in kindergarten yet and at the rate he was learning he was nearly beyond elementary school math. By kindergarten we were working with facts about exponents and logarithms, which students don't usually learn about until high school. I didn't have to tell Alex that when you multiply an expression like

$$(5^x)(5^y)$$

the answer was $5^{(x+y)}$. He figured it out like I was asking him for the sum of $2+2$.

I would look at him in wonder. But I was scared, too. I was scared that he would stop learning so rapidly. I knew that if his math skills continued to be as amazing as I was beginning to believe they were, they could be his ticket to a happy and independent life. And I didn't want to pressure him to learn more or push him to the point where he thought it was work and not fun. The last thing I wanted to do was turn him off on math. That didn't seem to be a problem, though. He loves math like nothing else.

I was thrilled at his math acumen, and I relished our math sessions. They were one of the few times other than the supermarket when we spoke to one another at any length. Those were special bonding times. I felt close to Alex then when we were doing math. We'd laugh. We'd actually hold an extended conversation. And I'd enjoy the wonder and happiness that gushed out of him.

Teaching him could also be tiring. At times I would try to hide a new concept from him to limit the scope of our math sessions, but his unceasing questioning and desire to tie up all loose ends would invariably propel us forward. Once he learned about negative numbers he was disturbed that the square root of any positive number was "ambiguous" because, for example, the square root of 9 can be 3 or −3. Therefore, I taught him about multiple roots and showed him how to graph functions and see those multiple roots. Then he would immediately say, "Well, what is the square root of −9?" Telling him there is no square root of a negative number did not sit well with him. And of course I knew how thrilled he gets whenever he discovers a new layer to the mathematical world, so I'd say, "It is $3i$, because i is the square root of -1. It is an imaginary number."

"OOOH! Imaginary numbers!"

Thus we entered the world of complex numbers. Transcendental numbers soon followed. Thank heavens I had a minor in math when I was in college or I could not have had a sustained conversation with my son.

Even in math, though, some concepts come more easily to Alex than others. His math strengths and weaknesses give further insight into how Alex sees the world.

Alex is in his glory when dealing with big concepts, getting to the heart of the underlying concept, mastering it, manipulating it, and seeing it from every perspective. He delights at finding interconnectedness in things. He is less facile when it comes to the step-by-step grunt work of math. At a young age he could set up a complicated mathematical expression to solve some problem but not be able to do the algebra to get the answer. In other words, as far as a standard math curriculum was concerned he could do the hard part of uncovering the structure of a problem but not the easy part of cranking through the numbers.

That's because seeing the whole picture is easier for him than breaking things down into steps. That's the reason he understood what a derivative and an integral are in calculus – and figured out the conditions for global and local optima – before he could do eighth grade algebra. He had a tougher time with long division than he had in learning the economic theory I taught my college students.

The root of this distinction lies in the difference between simultaneous (or holistic) and sequential thinking. Holistic thinkers look at the broad picture of things and see the underlying patterns. Sequential thinkers break things down into a series of small steps. For example, what would you do if someone handed you a piece of paper and a pencil and said, "Give me directions to your house." A sequential thinker will write out a series of instructions: take a right on Main Street, go two miles until you get to the third traffic light, make another right on Elm, and so forth. A simultaneous thinker will draw a map.

According to an evaluation done at the Sir Alexander Ewing–Ithaca College Speech and Hearing Clinic in 1993:

> Simultaneous processing involves learning from general to specific. Learners who are simultaneous processors learn best when given the whole picture first before teaching the pieces... Alex has demonstrated a tendency towards simultaneous processing...this can be used to help him process information. Simultaneous learning styles can be enhanced by structuring the way concepts or questions are phrased. Visual demonstration aids in the processing of verbal information (maps, diagrams, writing information as a supplement to information presented auditorily)... Autistic children have a tendency to learn things in unanalyzed chunks. This is demonstrated verbally when they use echolalia to learn or process language.

Most people can think both ways, usually with a strength in one type of thinking compared to the other. Alex is way on the holistic end. This can get him in trouble when no overall pattern is apparent. He doesn't know what details are important and he is always trying to synthesize all the information that confronts him. If this gets too overwhelming than he will just want to remove himself to a simpler environment where he can focus, like a laser, on something he understands. His solace is usually a math or science book.

The speech pathologists at Ithaca College helped us refine the way we presented information to Alex. But no path is straight. One idea they had to help us keep Alex focussed on a task was verbal mirroring.

Verbal mirroring is a technique where you describe out loud what another person is doing in order to focus their attention on their behavior. Alex could never stick to the task of getting dressed in the morning so we thought that would be a good place to first apply the latest weapon in our arsenal. Instead of yelling at him to hurry up we would go through the following:

"Alex, you are sitting on the floor. You are not getting dressed. You are playing with your sock."

Instead of getting upset at us for yelling, Alex soon started getting dressed. Eventually it was almost automatic. We'd only have to say, "Alex you are sitting and staring at the wall" and he would resume getting ready for school. We were happy and impressed. A major source of morning aggravation was alleviated. We decided to mirror him at other times.

It was time for dinner. I had asked Alex to come to the table several times but he was lost in thought in his room. I went upstairs, and stood in his doorway.

"Alex, you are sitting on the floor."

Then, like magic, quick as a bunny, he immediately started getting undressed. I never laughed so hard in my life.

22

Frame of Reference

↶

"Hey Simon, want to fly the airplane?"

Simon trots up to the control panel and scampers up into the pilot's seat. He grabs the throttle and starts making vroom-vroom noises, rapidly flicking buttons and switches with one hand while he rocks the steering wheel back with the other. His face doesn't reach the windshield. After a few minutes he's done, and moving on.

"Where are you going now?"

"To the fire truck!"

We yield the cockpit to some children waiting behind us at the Discovery Center in Binghamton. It is an actual World War II era cockpit and very cool. A few feet away is an old fire truck. Arranged in a circle around the inside of a single-story building are, among other things, a bank, a supermarket, and a diner, not to mention a bubble room. The center of the building has a climbing structure with an intricate array of tunnels and ramps.

Simon is dressed in red overalls with little trains on them. His rear end is puffy from the diaper he is wearing.

"Are you going to put on that firefighter's hat?" I ask.

His head disappears up to his chin. His fine, dark brown hair and hazel eyes hidden deep inside the recesses of the real-life fire helmet. The yellow rubber coat he's wearing reaches the floor.

"You look great, Simon!"

"Take it off!" There's an edge of panic that quickly disappears as I yank off the helmet and laugh.

"Yeah, I guess it's kind of too big, huh?" I say, not believing I forgot to bring my camera.

"It's for big kids. I'm gonna go up on the truck!"

Nanette is with Alex in the bubble room. We're doing our usual divide and conquer. I've got the easy job. With Simon you just go along for the ride.

"Want to switch?" asks Nanette.

"Sure. Simon is trying on shoes in the shoe store."

On the way home both boys fall asleep – a major accomplishment.

"Well, that was a good day," says Nanette.

"Yeah, but did you see the way those other kids play? Alex was really out of it. And there's only a couple of things he'll do there."

"Dan, he's always out of it."

"No he's not – not like that."

"Not when you're doing math with him, no. But how often do you see him with other children?"

"On the playground."

"But you're always right there playing with him. When do you see him side by side with other kids?"

I rarely did. When I came home it was just the family. We didn't socialize with others much.

"He's getting better," I said. "He's not terrified of other children. He's got his pronouns straight. You can have a conversation with him.'

"When was the last time you spoke with another four-year-old? You can have a better conversation with Simon than with Alex."

"Yeah, but Simon's really precocious when it comes to verbal stuff."

"A little, Dan, but not that much."

I didn't have a frame of reference. At least there wasn't one being thrust in my face every day. I would comfort Nanette when she started worrying about what would be with Alex. She constantly ruminated over unanswerable questions...Will he be able to live independently? Will he get married? Can he handle college? Will he ever have friends?

When I focussed on those questions I got upset, too, to the point of tears, but I didn't understand the point of dwelling on all of that. Why think so far ahead, I thought. We can only deal with today. Besides he was slowly getting better. I could see the growth. I didn't want to be forced to worry or feel bad. We were working hard with Alex. We weren't being complacent, so why work myself up when it wouldn't do any good? But seeing Alex amidst all the other kids at the Discovery Center was a bit jarring.

"You say how much better he's getting, but what you can't see is how other kids are growing more," said Nanette.

My isolation from other children – and my distractions at work – kept me less emotional. It allowed me to compartmentalize.

"You're so calm," she said, "maybe I am being too emotional. You're like Charla's husband. Charla says he only sees Hillary as Hillary. He doesn't know any other children. She has Down's syndrome but he just sees her developing from day to day. She wishes she could be like him, but she can't. She sees what other children are doing, and what Hillary is missing."

Every once in a while, though, it caught up with me, and when it did I struggled not to show I cried. I sometimes dumped my worries on people at work. That release was important, but oftentimes I was told that things didn't sound too bad. In a way that was what I wanted to hear, but I also grew indignant. "How do you know?" I thought. "What right do you have to tell me it's not as big a deal as I say it is?" Yet with family members I downplayed things.

"Hi, Mom."

"How's Alex? I worry so much about that little guy. My heart aches for him."

"He's doing much better, Mom. Really." I didn't want her to worry.

"That's so good to hear."

At work it was different. I'd say, "Alex and Simon are fighting like cats and dogs, all the time. They never do anything together, ever."

"All brothers fight," was the reply.

"Yes, but you don't understand. They have nothing in common. Simon gets frustrated and angry and Alex is oblivious. Or Simon pushes his buttons and he blows up."

"That doesn't sound all that different from my boys."

"It's a matter of scale! It's a matter of constancy."

I didn't know who to talk to, and yet I talked to everyone. I would bend the ear of anyone who would listen. Sometimes I would have to go to Nanette for comfort. In the end, she's the only one who 'gets it.'

"Hey, Nanno."

"Did you boys have a nice time?"

"Yeah. Did you and Simon have a good time at the birthday party?"

"Yeah, it was nice. The kids are really starting to play together. It's not just parallel stuff anymore."

"We went to the Belle Sherman playground. There were kids Alex's age. Nanette...I know you see it all the time, but...they were all playing and Alex was fixated on...they were laughing and talking and...like real buddies, you know?"

"I know."

"I...I don't want to start crying."

"Go ahead and cry. You're allowed to cry," she said, giving me a hug. "Well, sometimes, anyway. Just not when I'm crying, OK?"

"Oh, that's wonderful. Just wonderful."

23

Spreadable Fruit

♋

The summer of 1992 was coming to an end. Nanette and I took Alex and Simon on walks near Ithaca's many waterfalls and had picnics in the park. Ithaca is glorious in the summer, and the town is less populated than usual because most of the college students are still on break. There are concerts on campus, Birkenstocks on people's feet, and enough pollen in the air to choke a horse.

That whole summer Nanette and I had a gnawing sense of dread. Alex would be turning five in October and it was time for public school. Our experience at the Special Children's Center had been better than expected, and Alex had shown noticeable signs of positive development. The Special Children's Center, however, did not have a program for Alex now that he was aging into his school years. He would have to move on to what we perceived as the big, impersonal, bureaucratic public school system.

Alex was young enough to delay the inevitable event. In fact, we briefly considered holding him back a year. After all, his level of social maturity could easily warrant delaying kindergarten. However, academically he was already well past kindergarten and we feared creating even larger problems in the future by making the discrepancy between his intellectual skills and his classmates' even greater. Besides, we had considered some nursery schools and they did not seem right. Most were noisy, often bordering on chaos and filled with pretend play. Plus, they had no academics, which Alex craved. He probably would have been happy at a Montessori program that Nanette visited but only because they would have let him sit alone in the corner all day doing math. His math skills would have gotten more advanced, but this was hardly necessary. Social skills were what he needed. Reluctantly we registered him for kindergarten.

Prior to the school year, we had our first of what over the years would be numerous meetings with school officials. Alex's diagnosis mandated that we convene to determine his proper placement.

We arrived at the school board building early and were ushered into a drab waiting room with a pile of outdated education magazines strewn on a small coffee table. I am chronically early, and so have spent much of my life in waiting rooms.

Nanette and I reviewed our thoughts. We wanted Alex in a regular classroom. He needed to learn how to interact with the rest of the world, and we felt this could best be accomplished if he was with regular children. We also wanted him to get speech therapy in order to continue the work he started at the Special Children's Center, and to have an aide to help guide him through the day. In addition, we were nervous about his being bored. When Alex is bored he becomes less tolerant of the things that bother him and less able to learn how to deal with them. Therefore, we wanted to ensure he was challenged academically.

Our meeting time arrived and we were led to a conference room that was nearly entirely taken up by a large table. Seated around the table was a veritable army of staff – teachers, administrators, therapists, district personnel, school personnel, and a parent representative.

"Well," I thought, "This is either the Grand Inquisition or the Knights of the Round Table; we'll see which."

Everyone introduced themselves, and someone briefly summarized the information in Alex's folder. We made our case and convinced them that Alex should be in a regular classroom. Resources being what they were, it was unlikely that he would get an aide. They wanted to take a wait and see attitude. We went on at length explaining Alex's weaknesses and strengths, as well as his idiosyncrasies. The special education director at Alex's school actually complimented us on how well we described Alex. Everyone was personable and professional, and they all stressed the importance of having involved parents. We left with a false sense of security.

Our first inclination that things would not be so rosy was when we met with the principal at Alex's new school. We wanted to touch base with everyone so they would be prepared for Alex, and to ensure that he was assigned to the most appropriate teacher. We drove out to the school, which was a couple of miles from our house. Being summer, the school seemed deserted except for the main office where there was a flurry of activity. The principal was a very professional looking woman in her late forties, well groomed and polished.

"Well, welcome to our school. I hear you're thinking of registering Alexander for this fall."

"Thank you. That's what we wanted to talk to you about," I said, "You see, Alex has some special strengths and weaknesses that we thought we should discuss before school starts."

"All children do," she said cheerily.

"Yes, but you know that Alex is autistic, right?" asked Nanette.

"Well, the Special Children's Center seems to diagnose a lot of children that way, and we're not always sure we agree with them."

"We had him evaluated at Syracuse University, too," added Nanette.

"We just wanted to meet with Alex's teacher before school began and explain a little bit about him," I said.

"Well, our teachers usually like to make their initial judgements about a child by themselves. New parents are always concerned about their children adjusting to a new situation, but it always works out fine. It could be that Alex just needs to wait a year before starting school. That would give him some time to mature."

He is autistic, I thought.

"It's not just that," Nanette continued, "We are also concerned about him being bored, especially if we hold him back a year. You see, he is also very, very good at math…"

"Yes," she laughed, "Many of *these* children learn addition and subtraction facts before they get to school but often they don't really have the concepts down."

Like fractions, exponents, and probability, I thought. She doesn't think we know our own child.

Clearly, nothing we had to say would make a difference. They'll learn soon enough, we thought. We left feeling patronized and ignored.

The school scheduled a pre-registration screening that all children were required to go through, but they also included a visit with the speech therapist for Alex. Alex went through the screening easily – he likes tests. They are structured and he does well on the ones that test academic preparedness. He also likes to scrutinize their scoring systems.

Eventually, it was time to see the speech therapist.

"Hi, Alex."

Alex sat across the desk from the therapist. They were in a glass office with an open door. I sat outside, within earshot, looking in. Alex had already been through several testing sessions with speech therapists, and was fluent in the scoring systems for various standardized tests.

"Very good, Alex!" she said. "You did well on that test. You have a great vocabulary. Now let me ask you a few more questions." She held up a jar of fancy jelly. "What is this?"

"Spreadable fruit."

"What?"

"Spreadable fruit."

"Where'd you get that from?"

Alex pointed to the label and read, verbatim, "Spreadable fruit."

"Oh, yes, I see. You can read. That's very good, Alex! But if you didn't see the label and I asked you what this was, what would you call it?"

A pause. A quizzical look. Then, "Spreadable fruit."

After a few more minutes she finally elicited the response of "jelly" from him, after practically spoon feeding him the answer. She was then able to check "jelly" off her list. The true insight into Alex that could have come from that moment, however, was lost.

24

Diabetes

○3

My mother was a diabetic. She was first diagnosed in her late thirties but doctors told her she needn't worry about it until she was older. They were wrong. By the time Alex started elementary school in 1992, her disease had progressed to the point where worrying became a major part of her life.

"The doctor tells me I need to start shooting up insulin."

"I thought you could control it with diet and pills."

"Not anymore."

"Are you sticking to your diet?"

"Don't talk to me like I'm a child, Daniel."

When we got together I would see her eating things she was not supposed to eat. My sister Debbie – who is a nurse – would get really upset.

"Did you see Mom eating that apple pie? I warned her not to," she said.

"I tell her, too, but she gets mad at me. What are we supposed to do?" I asked.

"She says she has a crummy job and enough troubles and it's her main enjoyment in life. But she's being shortsighted. I've been telling her for years it is going to come back and haunt her."

My mom's eyesight started to worsen, and she began having difficulties at work. Eventually her doctor told her she could qualify for Social Security Disability Insurance. She was excited that she could finally stop working and do the things she wanted. Travel. Play Mah Jong. Volunteer for various organizations. My mom had always been a big volunteer – for her old synagogue, the PTA (Parent Teacher Association), and various clubs. At work, too, there were countless instances when she advised and helped people. Many times people sought her out. Technically, she was the manager of a credit union but she often also took on the role of counselor, dispensing advice, emotional support, and financial counseling to many of her clients. I think it was that unofficial part of her job that kept her going. I think losing that almost outweighed leaving the commute behind and the officious bosses and lousy working conditions.

"I hear they have laser surgery to help stop the retinopathy. They'll fix me up and I can finally do my own thing. Diane's living on her own now and I've got the house to myself. Who needs to go into that awful office?"

My dad's health, too, was not the best. He had suffered a major heart attack when he was 47 and was always concerned that it would end his life prematurely. When we visited my parents they always wanted to talk about their wills. They made Debbie and me promise over and over again that we would look out for Diane.

My mom brushed off the diabetes and my dad exercised every day, but they always thought about death. They moved into a retirement village even though my father said he planned to work until he dropped.

"You're in your fifties. Why do you talk like you're so old?"

"I *am* getting old, Daniel. Anyway, there's lots to do around here and we're close to the shore. I'm looking forward to it. This is retirement now. This is finally my time."

25

Off to School

ෆ

Caroline Elementary School, where Alex attended kindergarten and first grade, posed some real challenges for the staff. The students who attend Caroline are drawn from two very distinct populations. Half of them are the sons and daughters of professors and other professionals. A large chunk of the people who live in Ithaca work for either Cornell University or Ithaca College. The other half of the student body live in neighboring towns, many of which are dirt poor. Their parents are uneducated, and some of them live in homes without furnaces, floors, or electricity. Some children arrive at their first day of school being able to read, while others don't know their colors or even proper hygiene.

The school is racially homogenous but class differences run deep and are apparent to the youngest children. A first grade girl we knew was horrified when her teacher recommended speech therapy for an articulation problem. She didn't want to be removed from class with "those other" children.

Alex's academic abilities put him near the bottom of the triage list. Since he was not aggressive towards others or himself, his problems were not considered all that serious. Teachers were used to kids who had difficulties relating to other children. What they didn't realize at first was that unlike other poorly adjusted children, Alex needed explicit instructions on how to learn social skills. He couldn't be taught by example, or in any manner that was not systematic.

Luckily, the teacher chosen for Alex fit him well. She was an experienced teacher with over 20 years in the classroom. She was energetic but firm, and not easily ruffled. Her classroom had enough structure to keep Alex secure – she used a work station approach along the lines of Alex's pre-school experience – without a lot of arbitrary rules which can drive Alex crazy.

Unfortunately, like her principal, she didn't want to hear much from us – at least at first. She probably figured we were just one more set of parents in a long line of overprotective couples who had a hard time letting go of their special little one. We thought she'd learn. She did.

As each week went by, his teacher would come to us with a new discovery.

"He can read the instructions on the worksheets!"

"He already knows all the math I plan to teach this year and more."

"He is very resistant to changing activities, and has a hard time communicating with the other children."

"He has no ability to stay with the group."

"Sometimes he focuses like a laser beam, but sometimes he has great difficulty staying on task. And he doesn't seem to know how to play with his classmates."

We would nod. "Really?" Who would have guessed?

It was very, very annoying. She would talk to us, which was good, and her perceptions were accurate, but clearly everything we had told her at our first few meetings went in one ear and out the other. It was exasperating. Yet time and time again we were told of the importance of parental input. Nanette and I would look at each other in disbelief.

I soon became more than annoyed. I was angry. The clock was ticking on Alex's early years. Everything we read stressed early intervention. I felt a vague sense of powerlessness at school. Of course, at home we were continuing our never-ending tutorials, and helping Alex learn to deal with Simon.

Why didn't we press our thoughts on her harder? We weren't education experts, and at the time we were not sure exactly what should be done. And we learned from experience that making demands without a clear sense of what you were asking for could backfire.

At the beginning of the school year the school was looking for a parent representative for their Committee on Special Education (CSE). A federal law mandates that all children classified as having special needs must have an Individualized Education Program (IEP) filled out for them. This IEP lists goals for the coming year, the child's placement, and the services he or she requires – for example, speech or occupational therapy. This document is legally binding and is the main tool parents can wield in their struggle to get their children proper services.

At Caroline, IEPs were developed and signed during CSE meetings. These meetings were attended by the school psychologist, the classroom teacher, the principal, the special education coordinator, the school nurse, and anyone else providing services to the child. Regulations also required the presence of a parent representative.

Nanette and I figured we would learn a lot about the system and get to know the staff if we volunteered to be that representative. They allowed us to share the position.

Sitting in CSE meetings was an eye-opening experience. Some parents showed up with ideas, outside opinions, and an overflow of concern for their children. Some parents did not show up at all. The staff could generally predict when that would happen. They were always the parents of the poor children. Maybe it was because they could not get time off from work. Maybe it was because they were intimidated. Maybe it was because they had too many other things to worry about, or they didn't care. But sitting with the committee and having to acknowledge that we would have to start the meeting without the parent was always a sad experience.

A high percentage of children at Caroline had IEPs. It quickly became apparent that the staffing was inadequate. It also became apparent that the squeaky wheel got the grease, if for no other reason than that parents visiting the school could focus the staff's attention on their children. School personnel knew they would be held accountable.

Nanette and I also noticed something else. As well meaning as most teachers are, they are only human and it can be hard at times for them to completely separate their relationship with a child from their relationship with that child's parent. Aggravate, annoy, or pester a teacher and it can influence not only their willingness to communicate with you, but how they respond to your child. A good, caring relationship between teacher and child is a fundamental building block in a child's educational program. We've always tried to protect that and help teachers help Alex.

Alex's first teachers, with their unwillingness to absorb parental input unless they discovered a problem that led them to consult us, tested our ability to live by this rule to the limit. But Alex's teacher developed a good sense of how to deal with Alex, and by midway through the school year we were more relaxed. She ended up growing close to Alex and was key in making our mainstream efforts successful.

26

Such a Bright Boy

Cஐ

Through much of kindergarten the staff at Caroline were not convinced of the profound nature of Alex's social problems. That realization grew slowly, as they got to know him better and as the other children developed at a faster rate. What they did notice was his intelligence. Once again we heard the familiar refrain of "uneven development."

"He is such a bright boy. Once he devotes some attention to social things, he'll catch up quickly."

Alex was slowly becoming a celebrity at school. He started helping the fifth graders on his bus with their math homework. This made a big impression on people. Of course, sometimes he would lie, crying, on the bus floor for reasons the bus driver could not discern. And often the older children had to assist him with the mechanics of getting on and off the bus and finding his classroom, but everyone was very impressed by his math skills.

Alex was also a precocious reader. He was pulled out of his class by a reading specialist a couple of times a week along with a few other children who also could read. We thought this was a very good thing. We hoped Alex could make a connection with some of the brighter children if they were in a small group discussing something very specific. Talking about books could also reinforce the efforts being made to help him hold a conversation.

Alex's reading skills, however, were far advanced from the other children. That is, his ability to decode words was much farther advanced. His ability to understand the stories he was reading was actually quite delayed. This wasn't clear at first so he was put in his very own group, apart from the other children.

We did not know this for weeks. We visited the school one day and discovered this fact when the reading teacher proudly displayed the book Alex was working on. She was very excited to be teaching such a bright, little boy.

He could read already, damn it! And he read on his own, without being told to do so (at least non-fiction). What he needed much more urgently was to learn how to get along with other children. He needed to learn the concepts of personal space, social norms, compromising, and social cues. He needed to learn how to talk to children.

"Those things will just come with time, as he matures."

"Not with him! He is autistic. He needs to be explicitly taught. His intelligence is limited – contained. Yes, he is bright. Thank God he is bright. But he has deficits, too!"

His lack of social understanding eventually reared its head in the academic world. Alex clearly was missing the point of most of the storybooks he read. He had no problem with math and science books but fiction often puzzled him. His problem was that he could not relate to or understand any of the characters. He did not understand the motivation for their actions, their feelings, or their relationships to each other.

Some researchers believe that autistic people lack a "theory of mind." That is, they cannot conceptualize the world from the view from inside someone else's head. For example, there is a classic experiment that autistic children tend to fail that non-autistic children – even ones with cognitive delays – don't fail.

A subject is shown a picture of a young girl, named Sally. Sally is putting an object in one of two boxes. Then the subject is shown a picture of Sally leaving the room, followed by a third picture of a little boy coming into the room and switching the object to the other box. The final picture shows Sally re-entering the room. The researcher asks the subject to report which box Sally thinks contains the object.

Non-autistic children say the box she placed it in originally, because Sally was not present when the boy came in and made the switch. Autistic children usually think that Sally knows the correct location of the object. When asked why, they will say Sally thinks it is in that box because that is where the boy put it. The autistic children have a difficult time understanding that Sally doesn't know where the object is located because she wasn't in the room when the switch was made. It is not second nature for them to realize that they have a different set of knowledge and experience from Sally and therefore they know things that she does not.

Psychologists use studies like this one to conclude that autistic people have no theory of mind. Some autistic adults I know bristle at this conclusion. They claim it underestimates or misinterprets their ability to relate to others. They state that they have no problem with theory of mind if the mind they are being asked about is autistic. The problem, they claim, is in trying to understand the NT mind.

Alex definitely has this problem. He cannot understand people's motivations, their demeanor, or quite often, their point of view. When reading a storybook he has great difficulty following a plot. We saw *Star Wars* in the movies recently and he could not keep straight who were the good guys and who were the bad guys.

In fourth grade he read a book where a class was taking advantage of a very nice teacher. The teacher was then absent for a while and replaced by a very mean teacher. The children were relieved and happy when the regular teacher came back and treated her much better. In the last scene of the book, you see the mean teacher's clothes in the nice teacher's closet. They were the same person. The teacher had tricked the class and taught them to appreciate her.

Alex could not understand this. If the two teachers were actually the same teacher, then the class should know. And why would a nice teacher act mean? And how can you make that conclusion merely from seeing the mean teacher's clothes in the nice teacher's closet? Maybe the nice teacher stole them, or maybe the mean teacher sneaked into the closet and put them there. Maybe they owned the same exact clothes.

A first grader would have no problem with this book. Simon didn't. Alex was in fourth grade. For his own entertainment he was reading *Scientific American*, *Science News*, and *Discover* magazines with relative ease. A first grade piece of fiction was inexplicable.

It is jarring to have a conversation with someone – Alex or another very high-functioning autistic person, either in person or over the internet. They communicate complex thoughts, sometimes in a very articulate manner. They clearly are very intelligent and even perceptive. However, a subject will come up and you are shaken by the blind spot they have about how people interact or the difficulty they can have in managing what seems like the simplest things – like eating, paying bills, registering for classes, speaking with someone on the phone, or dealing with minor surprises at the last minute.

Alex can sometimes appear to be sassy and exaggerate a lot.

"OK, you told me to slow down. How slow should I move? Ten microns per second?"

"That's ridiculous, Alex. You know that's not what I mean."

"OK, so exactly what do you mean by slow?"

He doesn't know. Where's the line between slow and fast? Where's the line between good-natured teasing and ridicule? Where's the line between neat and messy? He doesn't know. Not knowing is incredibly frustrating. He probably knows how an internal combustion engine works, but that's a piece of cake. When can you touch someone's face and when is it not allowed? He doesn't know.

"How can he not know? He is such a bright boy."

Slowly, school officials were convinced that the social skills he lacked were serious and he wasn't going to grow out of his difficulties naturally. The first problem that became an issue was Alex's inability to stay with a group. This posed particular challenges at school. Often, Alex was lost "in transit." The class would line up to follow the teacher to lunch or the art room or music room. Like little ducklings, the kids would travel through the hallway to their destination. Upon arrival, Alex would be nowhere in sight. A few minutes later he would be found in a different hallway, reading some bulletin board, oblivious to the fact that he was no longer with his class. One time a little boy in his class who we knew rather well said matter-of-factly, "Alex got lost at school again, today."

Naturally this was a security threat. We were none too happy. The problem was "solved," though, by the teacher always reserving second place in line for him. The lead spot was too prime. That way she and all the other children could keep an eye on him. Even in fifth grade there was usually a child assigned to "Alex duty" to make sure he stayed with the class.

The habit of wandering away, or not feeling attached to a group, became even more disconcerting when we learned in first grade that Alex has extreme difficulty in recognizing faces. In fact, aside from his immediate family, there are probably only a handful of people he can recognize – even among people he knows and loves.

Our discovery of this fact was quite a surprise. We were planning Alex's sixth birthday party. He was born in October so this was about the fifth week into school. Alex wanted a bowling party. We told him he could invite eight children.

"Who do you want to invite?"

"I don't know."

"How about if we go down the class list and you can say 'yes' or 'no'."

"OK."

"Do you want to invite Ben?"

"Yes."

"Eric?"

"Yes."

"David?"

"No."

Eventually we got eight children to invite. A week went by and a few people had not called to RSVP.

"Alex, did anyone at school tell you they were coming to your party?"

"Yes. Four people."

"Who were they?"

"I don't know."

"What do you mean? You don't remember which kids told you they were coming?"

Alex's eyes started to water. His face got flush. "I don't know their names," he said, "Why don't these people wear name tags anymore?"

"Name tags? You mean, you don't know who the people in your class are?"

"No."

"Well, how did you decide who to invite?"

Puffing his chest out with pride, he said, "I chose RANDOMLY!"

Too stunned to laugh or cry I just buried my head in my hands. The party went fine, but at school the next week his aide started showing him pictures of the children and helping him identify who was who. He quickly learned the names associated with each picture, but he could never transfer that knowledge to the task of identifying someone in real life. He probably was remembering certain facts about the picture. John, for instance, was the guy in green putting Legos together.

Recognizing people close to him was not easier. A friend of ours came over for dinner one night and Alex, who is usually disinterested in our guests, immediately asked her to play a game and sat in her lap. He was about nine years old at the time. He was being very friendly towards her, which was nice but unusual. Then he said, "It's your turn, Grandma!"

"Grandma! That's not Grandma."

He quickly put his head down in embarrassment and waved his hands in front of his face.

"OK! OK!"

Our friend has approximately the same build as my mother, who was one of Alex's favorite people. She also had a similar hairstyle and hair color. Then again, she was also about thirty years younger.

Some people who are not autistic cannot recognize faces. This condition is known as facial agnosia, and can be very difficult to live with. We took Alex to a neurologist but he thought facial agnosia was not Alex's problem. He believed that Alex just doesn't focus on faces or find them important. That may be a major part of Alex's problem with facial recognition, but even when he concentrates he has difficulty. Possibly, he can't distinguish faces because he didn't learn the skill when he was young.

He does recognize Nanette, Simon, and me. However, that ability is fairly recent. Once Nanette asked him if he could pick her out in a group if she was sitting in the living room with a bunch of women. He said, "It depends what they look like."

I can't imagine going out into the world and not being able to recognize people, having each person who comes up to me and says hello being an unknown entity until I consciously decipher what their identity must be. The mere fact of not knowing who knows me and who doesn't and what the people who do know me expect of me would be extremely unsettling. To me, it would be like walking into a world designed by Edgar Allan Poe.

27

Mathematical Marvel

CB

A lex quickly advanced to factorials, combinatorial mathematics, and probability.

"Alex, if you have six people, how many arrangements of three people can finish in first, second, and third place if you had a race?"

A few seconds later, "120. You see, six times five times four."

"That's right. Because you can have six different people finishing first, but for each first place finisher you can only have five different people possibly coming in second and for each pair of first and second place finishers there are only four possible people who can come in third. Now, how about this one?"

He giggles.

"What if order didn't matter? What if you only cared about how many different groups of three people could be in the top half of finishers?"

This took a few more seconds.

"It would be 120 divided by 6. Twenty."

As usual, I was blown away. He was right, of course. You need to divide the first answer by the number of ways of arranging three people, which, by the same line of reasoning, is three times two times one. Basically, he had deduced, in less than five minutes, the formulas for the mathematical concepts of permutations and combinations.

One of my favorite math stories involving Alex happened when he was in second grade. Alex was perusing one of his many math books, and came across the following problem: "It is now 7 o'clock. What is the soonest time at which the hands of a clock will be directly on top of each other?" The answer is not 7:35, because by the time the minute hand gets to the seven the hour hand will have moved.

The way the math book wanted you to solve the problem was as follows: The minute hand moves twelve times faster than the hour hand. The hour hand is starting 35 minutes ahead of the minute hand. So if we let the number of minutes that must elapse before the two hands line up equal x, then:

$$35 + (1/12)x = x$$

because the number of minutes the minute hand must move is 35 plus the number of minutes the hour hand moves while the minute hand is trying to catch up, namely $(1/12)x$. This is how I solved the problem when Alex posed it to me. Basically, this is a high school algebra problem.

Alex, however, being a true mathematician, wanted to solve for the general case. He worked on this problem for quite some time in his room. He emerged with the following solution:

Pick any time. Let z equal the number of minutes it will take the minute hand to get to where the hour hand is now. By the time it does, the hour hand will travel a distance of $(1/12)z$. Now it will take the minute hand $(1/12)z$ to get to where the hour hand has moved. By the time it does, the hour hand will have moved $(1/12)(1/12)z$. Continuing this sequence into infinity leads to the following expression for the number of minutes it will take the minute hand to catch up to the hour hand:

$$z + (1/12)z + (1/12)^2 z + (1/12)^3 z + ... =$$
$$z \sum_{n=0}^{\infty} (1/12)^n = z / (1 - 1/12) = z(12/11)$$

So basically, if you want to know how many minutes it will take for the hour and minute hand to be on top of each other starting at 4:00, you simply note that z at that time is 20 because the minute hand will take 20 minutes to get to the four (i.e., where the hour hand is now) and plug it into the expression $z(12/11)$ to get $240/11$, or about 21.8 minutes.

Alex sits hunched over on the floor or at the table, a well-tattered math book with peanut butter stains and frayed edges at his side. Maybe a motley collection of scrap paper is strewn in front of him. His perpetually dirty hands are awkwardly wrapped around a pencil, pen, or crayon as he feverishly writes down his calculations in a messy scrawl. He pays little attention to any lines on the paper, and will sometimes erase with so much force that the paper has little holes worn through. Giggling to himself, with his hand over his mouth, invariably making pen marks on his face and arms, he sets about solving math problems with glee. If he finds a particularly tricky problem – either in a book or in the unfathomable reaches of his mind – he will barely be able to contain himself. He will jump up and run over to us, sometimes laughing so hard he cannot speak.

The stories of Alex's analytical abilities are endless. When he was in kindergarten I tried to impress him with a story of Gauss, a famous mathematician, as a child. Gauss was asked to sum the integers from 1 to 100 and arrived at the answer in a couple of minutes while the rest of his class was busy computing away for hours.

"Alex, can you sum up all the whole numbers from 1 to 100?"

"Would that be 50.5 times 100, or 5050?"

"Yes, Alex, how did you get that?"

"Well, you're adding up 100 numbers and the average size of the numbers is 50.5."

So much for impressing him.

Alex also has a penchant for finding mistakes in books and on math tests. When he was about five or six he found an error in a math book. The book explained that the probability of winning the game Bingo by getting five in a row along the top line of your card with only five numbers being drawn is $(1/72)(1/71)(1/70)(1/69)(1/68)$. The author's reasoning was that you have a 1 out of 72 chance of getting the top number in the B column on the first draw. After that, you have a 1 out of 71 chance of getting the top number in the I column on the second draw because there are only 71 numbers left. Alex correctly stated, "That's not correct. That's the probability of getting that BINGO in order from left to right. The probability of it happening in the first five draws is $(5/72)(4/71)(3/70)(2/69)(1/68)$ because you can fill in that row in any order. You have a 5/72 chance of getting a number in the top row on the first draw, followed by a 4/71 chance of getting another number on the top row if you got a number on the top row on the first draw, etc."

The thing I find amazing is that he never assumes a book is correct. He must always verify what he reads by using his own sense of logic. I didn't learn to think that critically until I was in college.

His academic abilities go beyond math. They extend to science, economics, and anything with an analytical basis. One time we were visiting Hershey Park and he wanted to know why they charged one entrance price and then let you ride as many rides as you wanted to for no additional cost. He had thought you maximized profit by charging a price equal to the marginal cost of production. I mentioned to him that there was a famous article written by an economist explaining this phenomenon. In the case of a local monopoly (that is, when there is only one amusement park in town, or it is only feasible to spend the day at one amusement park) you can capture some consumer surplus by charging a single entrance fee. The explanation for this is complex, and it involved explaining demand curves and consumer surplus – concepts that my first year college students in economics often took a few lectures to grasp. Alex absorbed it in about 15 minutes.

But then Alex said, "Well, but different rides wear out at different rates. Shouldn't there be an additional fee depending on the cost of maintaining each ride?"

"A good question, Alex. But that article I explained to you was concentrating on a demand side effect. You're talking about a supply side problem."

"Well, if he was going to write an article about this, why did he only look at the demand side?"

28

Simon

⚘

I always wanted a brother. I imagined that the bond between brothers went beyond ordinary friendship. So when Simon was born I was thrilled that my boys would have each other. I envisioned the pair of them making their way through life like Tom Sawyer and Huckleberry Finn. For years, though, it seemed the brotherhood I fantasized about was not to be.

When we brought Simon home from the hospital Alex did not even seem to notice. Two-year-olds supposedly get jealous of new siblings, or at least bristle at the accompanying reduction in attention. Not Alex. Simon entered our family with the barest of ripples.

At first we thought this was a good thing – an anticipated source of tension never materialized. However, as time went on, Alex's indifference began to hurt Simon.

When Simon was a baby, his gaze followed Alex around with awe. Everything Alex did fascinated Simon. By the time he could crawl, Simon was intent on playing with his big brother, but Alex wanted nothing to do with him. Simon was an annoyance. He wasn't interesting. He wasn't funny. He almost wasn't even there.

Again and again, Simon's efforts to approach Alex were rebuffed. Simon alternated from constant entreaties for Alex's attention to outright anger. He could take only so much rejection before he lashed out. And we couldn't blame him. Our hearts went out to him. All he could understand was that his big brother – the person in the world he most wanted to play with – wanted nothing to do with him. Amazingly, though, after a couple of days of being angry he was ready to steel himself for an attempt to reach out to Alex.

"Do you believe this, Nanno? Simon's trying to make friends again."

"More power to him. I would've given up by now."

The problem was Alex disliked Simon's way of playing. *Who* he was playing with had no appeal, it was only *what* he was doing. The one activity that both boys consistently liked to do was molding things out of play dough, so Nanette made batches and batches of home-made play dough. Alex made letters. Simon made a mess. But at least they were side by side and that made Simon happy.

We tried other ways to get them to play together, but when we did Alex grew frustrated. He'd get upset because he could not grasp the fact that Simon did not have the intellectual capability at the age of one or two to play the board games that Alex was then capable of playing. Alex would be mad that Simon would not play Monopoly. The fact that Simon did not even know the alphabet was unfathomable to Alex.

By the time he was three, though, Simon displayed an amazing ability to engage Alex – at least for brief periods.

"Alex, do you want to play hide-and-seek?"

"No!"

"Daddy, Alex won't play hide-and-seek with me."

"Alex, honey," I said gently, trying to keep the edge of desperation out of my voice, "Why don't you just try it for a little while. You might think it is fun?"

"No. I don't like that game."

"Alex," said Simon, "We could play for *points*!"

Alex's head snapped around, his eyes wide and his face expectant.

"POINTS?"

"Yeah, we can play for points!"

Brilliant! Why didn't I think of that? Alex was attracted to any systematic activity, and points implied a system and the chance to strategize.

Simon ran around the yard aglow from his achievement, his eyes alive with enthusiasm. Simon is short and thin but bursting with energy. He has hazel eyes and a round face. When he was younger his hair was dark, bordering on black.

"You got five points!"

"Wow," Alex exclaimed, "I'm winning 12 to 4."

"OK, Alex, that hiding place was worth 100 points!"

"That's surprising. I didn't expect to get that many points. Why is it 100?"

"It just is. What's the score?"

"I'm winning 112 to 4."

Simon was on a roll. I could see the wheels spinning inside his head, desperately trying to hold on to Alex's attention. He reminded me of a surfer riding a wave, knowing the exhilaration would last only so long, trying to maintain his balance.

The problem, alas, was that Simon at the age of three could only maintain the charade of a system for so long.

"One million points!"

"What? That makes no sense! How can that be worth one million points? What's the system?"

The game was over. Once again, Simon's enthusiasm got the best of him. The emperor had no clothes. Alex stormed off, and Simon cried. The image of my two sons playing and laughing together slowly faded, as I took Simon in my arms to comfort him.

Simon looked longingly at other siblings as they played together. To achieve even a brief moment of that kind of togetherness Simon had to plot and scheme, cajole and create. His ability to do so was breathtaking, even though I knew, with the inevitability of a Greek tragedy, that Alex would discover Simon's rules were inconsistent, incomplete, and at times nonsensical.

Simon honed his empathic skills. We knew several people who had children with developmental problems. Simon never knew what to expect when he met another child. He had to scope them out and try to understand them on their terms. Unlike most little kids, he was consistently asked to focus on what others felt.

Simon is a shy boy – usually quiet and reserved when he meets people – but once comfortable in a new social situation he becomes very well liked and usually at the center of things. Partially, this is because he has learned how to read people and deal with them. He takes great pride in his abilities. For example, he always knows what to buy each child for his or her birthday and is always pleased to report that his gift was the child's favorite. He is always socially "in the know," and he is usually very understanding of children with problems. Simon misses many of the things he'd like to do with his brother, but I like to think that there are traits that Alex has inadvertently helped him acquire.

The world fits Simon like a glove. He is smart, but he fits in with the other children. He enjoys sports, he makes friends easily, and every kids' event or venue that we visit seems tailor-made for him. He's an all-American boy. Of course, he doesn't see it that way. At times, he has problems with friends; he is concerned about being "cool," and he can stress out over spelling tests. He keeps a journal to record his days, and he is very serious about it. Compared to Alex, Simon glides through life, but that is not a fair comparison. I have to continually remind myself that his problems are real and big and important.

Appreciating Simon's problems with the same gravity as we do Alex's – and recognizing that growing up for anyone, no matter how "normal" or well-adjusted is a rocky journey – can be easy to forget among the swirl of worries and concerns surrounding Alex. But every once in awhile, Simon brings them home, and reminds us that having Alex as a brother can give them their own particular twist.

"I can't start kindergarten. I don't even know how to multiply yet." Or, "I don't know. Why don't you ask Mr Brain?"

We try not to fuss over Alex's accomplishments in front of Simon – winning the school spelling bee or acing every single exam – but they are apparent to Simon nonetheless. We try not to have long discussions about academic subjects that are well over Simon's head in front of him, but they are the only kinds of conversations I can have with Alex, and I love them.

Simon receives his report card and pores over it.

"I'm above grade level in reading, but only at grade level in math. By the end of the year I'll be above grade level in math, too."

"Don't worry so much about grades, Simon. You are a smart, talented, wonderful boy with a great report card. Just do your best."

When Alex walked up to elementary school, everyone said "hello." The children find it a challenge to elicit a response. Bringing Alex to school makes you feel like a celebrity, especially since the *Washington Post* did a front page story on him after he aced the National Mathematics Olympiad. The funny thing, however, is that Alex has no idea who is saying "hello" to him. Everyone knows him but he knows almost no one.

We enter the school and I glance at Simon. What is he thinking? How does it feel when kids rush up to him and say, "Hey Simon, can you get your brother to help me with my math homework?" Simon is proud of Alex but the usual sibling rivalry is still there. How can he compete in a world that gives awards for tests but not for being a well-rounded person?

"Simon, you are a great guy. You're smart. You're good at sports. You're kind. You have friends. You like art. You know how to take care of yourself. Alex is super, super good at math but he has trouble with lots more things than you do. Things that don't show up on tests."

We talk about autism. I don't know how much Simon understands but I don't want him to feel responsible for Alex or to baby him – not for his sake or for Alex's. I admit there are times I feel the urge to explicitly use Simon as a teacher's aide, but I must resist. Simon has enough to worry about growing up. Besides, by being a regular brother Simon has helped Alex immeasurably in learning to deal with other children.

Some things, though, I cannot tolerate.

"Were you laughing at him?"

"No."

"Come over here." I draw Simon away from his friend. "You were mimicking him. I saw you. You NEVER make fun of Alex! Especially in front of your friends. I know he can act weird sometimes. I know he can be a pain. If you don't want to play with him when your friends are around, fine. You don't have to include him all the time. But you don't make fun of him. You are brothers. You need to stick together. That's what family does, do you understand?"

Simon does understand. Babysitters tell us that Simon teaches them how to deal with Alex. Friends and family tell us how Simon takes charge and looks after him. When Alex gets upset about noise or the fairness of rules or any one of a number of his pet peeves, Simon explains what is going on. He will set up activities to entertain Alex and act as an intermediary and interpreter. He even makes sure Alex gets the food he likes.

I've also seen Simon stand up to his friends the few times they start to ridicule Alex. Simon has burst into tears telling me about children who have ridiculed Alex. He has refused to play with a friend of his for weeks at a time when he catches the boy mimicking Alex. Yet, Simon fights with Alex, too. He demands that Alex meet him as close to halfway as possible, and of course at times he baits him and pushes his buttons. He's a little brother, after all.

His protectiveness of Alex has spilled over into other relationships, too. As my mother grew more debilitated by diabetes – a disease that slowly deteriorated almost every part of her but her mind – Simon started caring for her. When we left our children with my parents, Simon made sure to get things for her when she needed them, and always took into account the fact that she couldn't see or walk very well. My mother was a proud woman, and always tried to minimize her medical problems. Simon saw them anyway, and stepped in to help.

Often he tried to sneak his assistance without my mom knowing so that she wouldn't feel bad. Alex would come into the room holding a board game that required reading things on tiny pieces of paper. Simon knew his grandma couldn't handle that, so he would try to surreptitiously shoo Alex away and suggest a card game. Then he'd retrieve my mom's oversized cards with big print. My mother would play along and pretend not to notice what he was doing, and my dad would get the poker chips. Simon would deal for seven card stud.

"A pair of bullets...no help there...ooh, possible inside straight."

29

Careers

⍟

The summer of 1992 kept Nanette on the go. Summers are always difficult for us because of their inherent lack of structure. That year, Alex was five and Simon was soon to turn four. Camp was not an option for Alex; it would only be torture. The noise and confusion would terrorize him and no game would be played "properly" enough. Throughout elementary school, even when he got older, most games quickly descended into meltdown mode.

"When is it my turn to kick the ball?"

"Whenever it comes your way, Alex. You have to go after it."

"OK! There are four people. How can I make sure I kick the ball one-fourth of the time?"

"You can't, Alex. That's not the way soccer works…Alex?"

By this time Alex was running wildly around the yard. His face was panic stricken. Wildly, he threw his body at the ball, as if getting to it was hopeless.

"OK, I'll just throw myself at the ball at two meters per second and break my leg!"

Sending Alex to camp would be like sending someone on crutches to run with the bulls at Pamplona. He'd quickly be overtaken, overwhelmed, and gored. Instead, Alex went to Camp Nanette. Her never-ending orchestration of games, projects, and carefully crafted outings was back in full swing.

As a professor, the summer provided me with plenty of flexibility. We could have lunch together on campus, and I could come home in the late afternoon and work at night. But summer is also the time to make headway on research projects that get interrupted during the school year by office hours, faculty meetings, and grading papers. I was trying to make significant progress on an annual report to the funding source for my special needs adoption project. The pressure of publish or perish that had lurked in the back of my mind was inching its way forward. My tenure decision would be coming in a couple of years and it would probably be a squeaker if I didn't put my nose a little closer to the grindstone.

The tenure decision for junior faculty in my department usually came in the sixth year but since my project included collecting a large amount of primary data – unusual for an economist – I had been granted a one-year extension. Still, the thought of my upcoming tenure decision unsettled me. On the one hand, I might get granted tenure and end up staying in Ithaca – at my first job – for twenty years. As much as I liked it at Cornell, I was uncomfortable with that prospect. On the other hand, I might not get tenure and be forced to uproot my family. There was no guarantee we would end up in a better place.

My career path was inescapably entwined with Nanette's career, and as Simon neared kindergarten, Nanette started entertaining thoughts of going back to work. Unfortunately, Ithaca has limited opportunities for employment. Nanette had taken some classes towards getting certified to teach math in high school, but she was finding the idea less appealing. Her true interests lay in policy analysis.

A larger metropolitan area had more opportunities for both of us, and probably contained more resources or special programs geared for children like Alex. Washington, DC seemed the best alternative to Ithaca. Being economists, there were lots of potential jobs. I decided to test the job waters there while the tenure ogre was not knocking at the door.

The job market for PhD economists is very structured. Basically, the best time to search for a job is at the American Economics Association meetings, which are held every year around New Year. Thousands of economists from all over the country descend on a city, filling hotels to present papers, attend meetings, and to hire each other. Most interviews actually take place in hotel rooms. Often the halls are filled with newly minted PhDs walking from room to room with sweaty palms and brand new briefcases. Setting up job interviews usually takes place in November. That left me a few months to wrap up some projects, finish some papers, and pull my vita together.

By the end of the summer Alex was ready to start first grade. He was anxious to get back to the classroom and substitute his amorphous summer days for the discipline of the school bell. Simon was off to pre-school at a program operated at Cornell. He was very excited to be a "big boy" and while he was a little intimidated the first week, he quickly became one of the gang. Nanette was set to begin student teaching, and the Cornell students rolled into town, their cars bursting with suitcases and boxes. The halls outside my office resumed their normal hum of activity. We were ready for the new year.

30

"Daddy, Look What I Can Do!"

❧

The beginning of a school year fills me with a happy anticipation and a sense of new possibilities. Everything is fresh. The slate is clean. Friends and colleagues you've barely seen during the summer now surround you.

The normal expectancy of the new school year, however, was tinged with trepidation. We had wanted Alex to have a full-time aide, but the school lacked the resources. Instead, Alex was scheduled to receive a limited amount of aide time in the afternoon, although he would still be pulled out for speech therapy. We also wanted Alex to have an aide on the playground, both because recess was his most vulnerable time, and because we felt it afforded an aide the most opportunities to facilitate interaction between Alex and some of his peers. We advocated for that all year, but again, there simply wasn't enough staff. We kept hoping that Alex's aides would function like adjunct teachers, but slowly we realized their main purpose was classroom management. The sense of "teachable moments" lost upset us greatly, but without being in the classrooms ourselves we felt powerless. Alex's aides didn't disagree with our objectives, but they didn't have much training.

Alex's IEP (Individualized Education Program) stated he should have more aide time. If push came to shove we had the legal firepower to demand it, but we were unclear if that was the best course of action.

Realistically, we didn't know how much more we could get in terms of quality help through confrontation rather than working with the staff. As the year progressed, Alex became more of a disruption and the school was motivated to rearrange their schedules to give him more aide time. However, instead of having one aide who stayed with him all day he had multiple aides who rotated turns with him throughout the day. That was not made clear to us for weeks. When we found out we threw up our hands in despair. Working with Alex – helping Alex – required getting a feel for how his mind works. Shuffling aides around made them more like babysitters. And there was nothing in Alex's IEP about a single aide, only that there would be an aide available for him. That limited our bargaining power and taught us the need to be specific on future IEPs. The aides kept order in the classroom, but to be an effective interpreter for Alex, a person needs to develop an understanding of exactly what is difficult for him. That takes time. To make matters worse, one of his aides was not a native English speaker. She was a charming person, but she had a heavy accent and did not speak proper English. Alex had problems understanding her, which added to his frustration and isolation. Given that speech was a problem for him, we felt she was an inappropriate choice. Nevertheless, she was the only aide available. In fact, she was a parent volunteer.

Alex's social learning disabilities and his inability to fit in with the other children and function cooperatively in the classroom became more apparent. His behavior could not be sloughed off as immaturity or the uneven development of a brilliant mind.

We met with the CSE to discuss a course of action, but Alex was unusual and there was no clear path.

Through our own research we learned about a "social skills" curriculum developed by some university professors. It consisted of material and lesson plans designed to teach children how to interact with peers in different situations. Lip service was given to incorporating these materials, but it required special training. The school was overrun with children requiring special attention. CSE meetings alone ate up huge chunks of staff time. Little time was left for developing new programs even though Alex didn't fit the old. After attending meetings and filling out IEPs, the school psychologist had very little time for actually working with children. She met with Alex for awhile and tried to teach him how to interact with another person. In a one-on-one setting, Alex made some progress having a conversation and undertaking a structured activity with someone else, but he never was able to generalize those skills to a broader context. He needed hands-on, in-class assistance. Assistance that just wasn't there.

Alex's growing verbal skills began causing problems for his teacher. Alex demanded an explanation for everything. Anything that seemed illogical or unfair elicited fits of despair and indignation. Several times a week he was sent, in tears, to the principal's office to calm down after an outburst. Once, when Alex had been absent a few days, his teacher told us it was a shock to realize how much of her time and energy he sapped from her with his constant need for explanations.

Later that year when we knew we'd be leaving the school district, we asked to have Alex videotaped so we could show his new school what he was like. In the tape, Alex walks around the room with no real emotion on his face. He talks to no one and doesn't participate with the other children. Occasionally he approaches the blackboard to write a math problem or what appears to be random numbers. He isn't teary-eyed and scared like the boy Andy described when Alex was in nursery school, but there isn't much difference. He moved alone in his own world. I wanted so desperately to crawl inside that little boy's head. To know my son.

Around this time, Simon was blossoming into young boyhood, leaving toddlerdom behind. He had an impish smile and a vivid imagination, making up stories off the top of his head and rambling endlessly. He found a soul mate at school – a little elfish looking boy named Eli. When they played together they were totally in synch, whether battling with action figures, throwing stones in a creek, or creating messy, drippy works of art.

Simon told jokes. Simon supplied a never-ending stream of "kids-say-the-darndest-thing" quotations. Simon was attuned to the world. Watching him develop gave us a sense of how "off" Alex was at that age. We were incredulous that his problems weren't more notice-able to us in the first place. We felt stupid.

Simon had his problems, too, of course. For a long while he wanted to be included with a group of boys who played together at pre-school. He hung out on the outside and longingly watched them play. Even-tually he mustered the courage to join the group, though. By the end of the year, he was at the center of everything.

We also realized how smart Alex had been at an early age. I would tell Simon something, maybe the sound a letter makes or what number comes after nineteen, and be surprised when he didn't assimilate the information instantaneously. I consciously had to work on not display-ing impatience because I knew he was learning at normal speeds. I couldn't expect a repeat of the lightning-like learning of Alex. It took me a while to realize that Simon was also very bright, but "normal" bright, like me and Nanette.

Simon invited friends over to the house. He went to birthday parties. He smiled and said hello to people we met on the street or at the park. We found these things wonderful and even awe-inspiring, but our hearts bled for Alex because he was completely cut off from the common everyday experiences that we saw Simon having.

Alex's year in first grade was perhaps his worst. He started to slide backwards. I was immersed in my effort to find a new job, flying down to Washington for follow-up job interviews and trying to tie up projects that would probably have to end when I left Cornell. Nanette was student teaching and trying to finish all her certification require-ments. Our daily involvement with the school lessened and Alex started to suffer for it. In fact, this was the only period in Alex's school career thus far when children began being mean to him.

One night, Alex's class invited the parents in to come and see the results of a major project they had been working on. Children and parents mingled, looking at displays the children had worked on and "oohing" and "ahhing" over all the posters and dioramas set up around the room. I was standing a few feet behind Alex, who had taken a math puzzle off the shelf and was fiddling with it. A little boy in his class tugged on his father's sleeve and brought him alongside Alex.

"Daddy, Daddy, look what I can do!" he said.

The boy leaned over and made a high-pitched noise in Alex's ear. Alex immediately lost his composure and started to scream and cry. I looked on in disbelief, expecting the father to say something. He looked a little uncomfortable and then just moved away. His son followed him, clearly enjoying his little power play.

I was furious. I didn't say anything because I was in shock at the father's disinterest in what his son did to my son.

"Why don't you teach your son a little human decency?" I thought to say, but too late. I comforted Alex but my thoughts strayed to my sister Diane. Visions of the torments she suffered throughout the years flooded through me. Kids hurled rocks at her as she walked home from school. The girls in her gym class surrounded her in the locker room and whipped her with towels. The other children teased her mercilessly or gave her the cold shoulder or bumped into her in the hallway to provoke her as she went from class to class. And all because she was different. I couldn't live with that happening to Alex. He was more defenseless. This was no time to slack off. That little boy screeching in Alex's ear was a call to action.

I spoke with Alex's teacher but she said she didn't observe things like that happening in the classroom. Maybe she didn't see them, but I didn't believe they didn't happen. How else would that little boy know exactly how to set Alex off? It obviously hadn't reached the horrors of my sister's school years, but we needed the school's help to make sure it never did.

The one thing that protected Alex was his intellect. Not because he used it to deal with other children, but because even at a very young age other children were awed by it. His skill in math earned him respect and keyed children into the fact that Alex was not clueless about everything and so could not easily be pigeon holed.

When Alex was in first grade, one of the fifth grade classes announced a school-wide contest. Each class was to submit as many ways as they could find to make change for a dollar. The class in each grade with the most ways of doing so would win a special calendar designed by the class sponsoring the contest. When the contest was announced over the loudspeaker, Alex's class shouted, "We're going to win! We have Alex!"

Alex got to work immediately and soon figured out a systematic way to attack the problem. He filled up pages and pages with the different combinations. His writing was huge and sloppy and the papers were filled with smudged pencil, but he was proud of his accomplishment.

The day the winners were announced, Nanette just happened to be helping out in the classroom. The principal's voice came over the PA system.

"And now it is time to announce the winners in the change-for-a-dollar contest. In fifth grade the award goes to Mrs A's class with 240 ways. In fourth grade, the award goes to Mr B's class with 121 ways. In third grade, the class who got the most ways to make change for a dollar was Miss C's class with 70 ways. In second grade the winner, with 43 ways was Mrs D's class. And in first grade, with ALL 241 ways, was Mrs E's class! And a special commendation goes out to Alex Mont who was the only person to get every single combination of coins!"

Alex dropped onto the floor with a huge smile on his face. He started wriggling on the ground with glee. The kids in his room cheered and clapped. One of them suggested letting Alex keep the calendar but Nanette said no, because he won it as part of the class. Instead, the fifth grade class voted that Alex should receive his own personal copy. The school was abuzz with talk about this enigmatic little boy who could not stay with his class, could not recognize a soul, cried for seemingly inexplicable reasons, but sure could count.

31

"Don't Mourn for Us"

ℭℬ

Our lives became consumed by autism and special needs education. We attended CSE meetings. We read books. We joined the Special Needs Advisory Committee set up by the school superintendent to provide an advocacy voice for special needs children. The Ithaca school district was dominated by overachieving professor parents and their precocious children. The superintendent thought an official organization that tried to rally parents of special needs kids, many of whom were economically disadvantaged, would help their concerns get as much attention as the parents of children labeled as gifted and talented.

Sally from the Special Children's Center called us to ask if we'd be willing to speak at a conference she was organizing. She said they were putting together a panel of parents of autistic children.

"Who would be the audience?' asked Nanette.

"Well, the conference is primarily for local educators to learn about autism, but we're also inviting other parents. Basically, we just want you to talk about Alex, the challenges you had with him, and how things have changed since he was diagnosed and you started learning about autism."

There were two other panel members, one of whom had a child similar to Alex, and another whose child was much lower functioning. Her daughter barely spoke, showed no emotion, and often displayed no evidence that she even knew who her parents were, let alone was emotionally bonded to them. Nanette and I almost felt guilty talking about our challenges.

People were very receptive to what we had to say and soon many people were calling us for advice and support. The most disturbing thing to me, though, was the number of women who complained about how resistant their husbands were to the diagnosis. We even met a couple of women whose husbands ran out on them once it became apparent that their child was autistic.

It became clear to us and to our friends with autistic children that we needed a more formal organization to reach out to other parents. We founded an organization called HiFAN (High Function Autistic Network) to serve as a source of support for parents like us. The Special Children's Center referred parents to Nanette and me like they had referred us to others. And other people found us, too.

"Hi, are you Daniel Mont?" said a wiry man in his early forties standing in my office doorway. He had black hair and a slightly graying mustache.

"Yeah, come on in and sit down. Are you the father I spoke with on the phone?"

"Yes. I'm glad you could see me. I was told you recently went through this."

"Your son was just diagnosed?"

His lips trembled a little. "Yes. He's three. I'm not sure I totally believe this. I didn't expect this to happen. I mean…and we're going back to California at the end of the week. I'm on sabbatical right now."

"It's a real shock."

His face radiated dismay and concern. It triggered memories of being in the waiting room with Nanette, hearing the word "autism."

"How old is your son?" he asked.

"He's six. He's in first grade. He's mainstreamed in a regular class."

"I never expected this. Autism! I don't know if I believe it…My son talks to me!" he said, getting agitated.

"So does mine. Look, here are some books you can read. Autistic people fall in a wide range."

Being a professor he snatched them up.

"Thanks." He started leafing through them, and then looked up. "Will he have a normal life?"

"You're asking me? All I know is you have to focus on the next thing you can do to help your son, and that he is the same kid he was before they slapped a label on him. You need the label. It gets you services and tells you where to go for help, but it's easy to let it overwhelm you."

He fidgeted and fought back tears.

"I'm in the political science department. I teach at the University of California...International stuff."

"Uh-huh."

"So these books are good? I'm leaving at the end of the week."

"Take them and mail them back to me."

"Right. I'll do that."

Sometimes the phone would ring at night and I'd hear Nanette talking to some obviously sobbing mother. We got calls from strangers, friends, and friends of friends. We met with HiFAN and blew off steam. We met with teachers and tried to explain Alex to them.

"We tried putting Alex in the fourth grade math class to give him something of a challenge, but he had a tantrum. He said the work was too hard," she said smugly.

"Really?" That didn't seem possible. "What were they doing?"

"Magic squares."

We looked at the assignment. He was supposed to fill in a four-by-four grid with numbers and make sure each row, column, and diagonal added up to the same number.

"He said this was too hard?"

We got a look back that said, "He's not as smart as you think. See, we do have things to teach him."

Later that night I asked Alex about the worksheet. He burst into tears. After some questioning I realized the problem. Alex was unwilling to do the worksheet by trial and error, making little adjustments as he went along. That was what was expected and what the other children did. Alex had been attempting to derive an algorithm for solving this general type of problem. That task was much, much more difficult and beyond his capabilities. He thought it was unreasonably hard. I agreed that what he was attempting was too difficult. I suggested the trial and error method, but he was uninterested. I explained this to his teacher but she gave me a blank look.

"Well, how could he be doing high school math, if he can't even do a fourth grade enrichment worksheet?"

Explaining Alex to the world – his strengths or weaknesses – was difficult. Sometimes we weren't sure we understood him ourselves. We needed someone to help us understand Alex better so we could better serve as his liaison with the rest of the world.

A friend in HiFAN told me about a listserve on the internet where people wrote to each other about autism. Some of the participants were health professionals. Others were teachers, and still others were parents of autistic children.

"And some," she said, "are autistic people themselves. Adults."

"Autistic adults!? Writing about autism?"

I was excited and intrigued.

"They can be angry, but some of them are very articulate and insightful," my friend continued. "They have jobs or are in college."

Armed with the internet address for the autism listserve maintained by Syracuse University and the instructions on how to join, I went to my office and closed the door. My office at Cornell was tucked away in the corner of an out-of-the-way hallway. Formerly part of a small library, it had a wall full of built-in bookcases. The lone window opened out on a small balcony that overlooked some woods. The sounds of Simon's pre-school – which was in the basement of my building – sometimes wafted uphill and into my office on nice days.

I threw my things down on my desk, turned my chair to face the computer table, and flicked on my machine. I sent an E-mail message to the listserver that automatically registered me to receive postings made to the list. I checked my E-mail hourly and slowly started amassing a collection of letters.

There, on my screen, were the hopes and fears of parents like me. Reports of research projects, various strategies for dealing with problems, and stories about experiences in schools all deposited themselves in my in-box. All were interesting, some were fascinating, and some were frustrating. For example, the lack of sophistication with which many people handled reports of scientific studies and the way they overgeneralized from a few anecdotes sometimes made my hair stand on end. What I appreciated most, though, was the energy, creativity, and emotional openness of many listserve subscribers. That, and the stories of how they coped, their achievements and setbacks.

The people I wanted to hear from most were the autistic adults. After a few days, a very articulate and insightful autistic man – a graduate student probably in his twenties or thirties – wrote in to give his take on a problem a parent was having with his child. My screen was filled with his message. The letters were little glowing lights that had traveled thousands of miles across wires and through various computers to reach me, alone in my office. I touched the screen.

Alex speaks more now, but back then we had no real conversations other than about math. We connected over some things but I knew we were different from each other in fundamental ways. How different? I didn't know. What did he think of people? Was he sad or scared? Did he care about the things that NT people care about? What could I expect from him in the future? The uncertainty of knowing none of these answers created a distance between me and Alex, at least in my own mind. Can you ever really know another person? I don't know. But as much as I love my son, I know there is much about him I don't know.

These autistic people writing in to the listserve were my window into understanding Alex. Of course they were different from him. Diagnosis or no diagnosis people are not clones of each other. Nevertheless, they had a connection with him that I could not have. And they were older, and could talk about themselves. I devoured everything they wrote.

The most powerful entry I read was one of the first. Many parents had written in about their grief – how sad they were for their children. Others had written about possible "cures" for autism – ranging from restricted diets to specialized programs to playing with dolphins. They reported how hard they were working to rid their children of the curse of autism.

The autistic people on the listserve were furious. Some NT people couldn't understand why they were so upset, or simply dismissed what they had to say. Maybe some of them felt that autistic people could not comprehend how wonderful it is to be NT.

One autistic man sent in an essay he wrote that changed Nanette's and my outlook overnight.

"Nanno, I brought home something for you to read. It came in over the autism listserve."

"What?"

"It's an essay called 'Don't Mourn for Us' written by this autistic guy who writes in a lot."

"'Don't Mourn for Us'?"

"Yeah. He says he's angry about people feeling sorry for themselves and for their children because their kids are autistic."

Autism is not some deficiency or disease that is superimposed on top of a person, he said. An autistic person is who he is because he is autistic. It defines his very essence. To "take away" his autism would be to change his personality, the way he thinks and relates to the world. To fight for a "cure" is to fight to destroy who he is. Even talking about a cure is, in fact, a way of invalidating his worth as a person.

The essay I showed Nanette made a profound impression on us. It fundamentally altered our outlook and even added a little richness to our relationship with Alex. To this day, Nanette keeps a copy of it in her desk drawer at work. The essay was published the next year in the first issue of Autism Network Internationals' newsletter, *Our Voice* (Volume 1, Number 3, 1993). Here are some excerpts from that essay:

Don't Mourn for Us

by
Jim Sinclair

Parents often report that learning their child is autistic was the most traumatic thing that ever happened to them. Non-autistic people see autism as a great tragedy, and parents experience continuing disappointment and grief at all stages of the child's and family's life cycle.

But this grief does not stem from the child's autism itself. It is grief over the loss of the normal child the parents had hoped and expected to have...

I invite you to look at our autism, and look at your grief, from our perspective:

Autism is not an appendage

Autism isn't something a person *has*, or a "shell" that a person is trapped inside. There's no normal child hidden behind the autism. Autism is a way of being. It is *pervasive*; it colors every experience, every sensation, perception, thought, emotion, and encounter, every aspect of existence. It is not possible to separate the autism from the person – and if it were possible, the person you'd have left would not be the same person you started with...

Therefore when parents say,

> I wish my child did not have autism,

what they are really saying is,

> I wish the autistic child I have did not exist, and I had a different (non-autistic) child instead.

Read that again. This is what we hear when you mourn over our existence. This is what we hear when you pray for cure. This is what we know, when you tell us of your fondest hopes and dreams for us; that your greatest wish is that one day we will cease to be, and strangers you can love will move in behind our faces.

Autism is not an impenetrable wall

You try to relate to your autistic child, and the child doesn't respond. He doesn't see you; you can't reach her; there's no getting through. That's the hardest thing to deal with, isn't it? The only thing is, it isn't true.

Look at it again: you try to relate as a parent to child, using your own understanding of normal children, your own feelings about parenthood, your own experiences and intuitions about relationships. And the child doesn't respond in any way you can recognize as being part of that system.

That does not mean the child is incapable of relating *at all*...

It takes more work to communicate with someone whose native language isn't the same as yours. And autism goes deeper than language and culture; autistic people are "foreigners" in any society. You're going to have to give up your assumptions about shared meanings. You're going to have to learn to back up to levels more basic than you've probably thought about before, to translate, and to check to make sure your translations are understood. You're going to have to give up the certainty that comes of being on your own familiar territory, of knowing you're in charge, and let your child teach you a little of her language, guide you a little way into his world...

Yes, that takes more work than relating to a non-autistic person. But it *can* be done – unless non-autistic people are far more limited than we are in their capacity to relate...We spend our entire lives doing this. And then you tell us that we can't relate...

Yes, there is a tragedy that comes with autism: not because of what we are, but because of the things that happen to us. Be sad about that, if you want to be sad about something. Better than being sad about it, though, get mad about it – and then *do* something about it. The tragedy is not that we're here, but that your world has no place for us to be...

...say to yourself: "This is not my child that I expected and planned for. This is an alien child who landed in my life by accident. I don't know who this child is or what it will become. But I know it's a child, stranded in an alien world, without parents of its own kind to care for it. It needs someone to care for it, to teach it, to interpret and to advocate for it. And because this alien child happened to drop into my life, that job is mine if I want it."

> If that prospect excites you, then come join us, in strength and determination, in hope and joy. The adventure of a lifetime is ahead of you.

The adventure of a lifetime. That much was true. I was blown away by Jim's piece, but I felt better for Alex, too.

Autistic people I know feel that autism has advantages. Autistic people do not immediately buy into social norms and conventions without thinking about them. Not only because at times they can't understand them, but sometimes because they see them for what they are, little rituals people use to feel a part of the group. Sometimes pointless, and sometimes painful to others. Their lives are not consumed by worry about what others think, a silly exercise as they often see it. They believe they can be freer to express themselves as they are. And being able to look at the world from a different point of view allows them to offer the world something exceptional. Articles have been written suggesting that many famous, creative people are, to some degree, autistic, from Albert Einstein to Bill Gates. I don't know if that is true. I do know that Alex's autism, while hampering him in the social realm, also makes him extremely creative in other ways. He does not assume as much about situations before going into them because he is not programmed to expect anything in particular, or what he expects is very different from the world he finds. This makes it easy for him to get overloaded in many circumstances because he doesn't have the internal sieve most people use to focus only on what is important at that moment. However, that sieve can sometimes function as blinders. In math and science, where he is most at ease, it is often startling to see how quickly he can find an easy solution to a problem precisely because his mind sees things from different angles. His train of thought is not as easily directed in a particular manner by the implicit assumptions most people make.

Nanette once said, "He thinks outside the box because he doesn't realize there is a box."

"Don't mourn for us," they said. They were happy with who they were. We cry for them because we can't imagine being alone.

"We like being alone. We don't need people like you do."

I wrote in to the listserve that I was worried about skipping Alex a grade in school. He would be more out of touch socially, I thought, even if he were less bored.

"People didn't skip me in school for the same reason," someone wrote. "But what was the point? I had nothing to do with the other children anyway, and the older children could better appreciate my strengths."

Related to this notion of autism being at the core of who they were, was their widely held preference for being called "autistic people" instead of "people with autism," or in the words of one particularly politically correct reference I ran into, "people carrying the label of autism."

"People with autism" denotes that autism is separate from what makes them a person; it is an add-on type of thing. Many autistic people prefer simply being called "autistic people" because that usage implies that autistic is the type of person they are, not something they have.

Reading letters from autistic people jolted me. I didn't agree with all they had to say, but their perspective was fresh and informative. I was also heartened by their strong sense of self and their camaraderie with one another. The level of independence some of them achieved made me more optimistic about Alex's future. The jolting part, though, was how articulate and perceptive they could be one moment when talking about themselves or their service providers, and then how clueless they could be about the motivations and actions of some NTs the next. Or how they could be successfully writing a PhD dissertation while being unable to cook for themselves, or deal with the daily transactions of life.

I wish I could provide you with more specific examples, but I cannot. I am morally obligated not to. The best listserve I have belonged to – and I have since been on several similar sites – is run by Autism Network International. A policy of that group is that nothing written there can be used or repeated elsewhere. They want their privacy and they do not want to be used as laboratory specimens. I've been very careful in this book when reporting about autistic people or internet discussion groups to make sure that everything I've said I learned from other sources, as well. The examples of internet postings come from other listserves.

Autism Network International also sponsors a conference for autistic people, their friends, and families. The conference runs the way they wish everything ran. For a few days they can live stress free, make connections with others, and learn and enjoy themselves in what to them is a natural environment.

When you register for this conference you get to decide what color badge you want to wear. A red badge means no one is allowed to approach you or speak to you. A yellow badge means only those people who know you well are allowed to do so. Perfumes and loud noises are not allowed. The food is bland. No sensory overstimulation here! Many sessions are run by autistic people. The brochure ensures that this conference is not like others that overload you with non-stop activity. Plenty of time is built in for you to go off by yourself and do nothing, if you wish.

Alex is always leery of "events." When we showed him the brochure for this conference, he nodded and immediately agreed to attend.

"I want to wear a yellow badge."

32

Moving to DC

♋

By March of 1994 I had accepted a position with the Congressional Budget Office in Washington, DC. I was excited about my new job. Change energizes me, and I love the idea of fresh starts. Furthermore, this was an important step for me. My entire adult life had been spent in academia. For years I was studying, writing, and teaching about public policy. Now I had a chance for a ringside seat. My first assignment was researching the impact of immigration on the nation's welfare programs. Before long I was briefing Congressional committee staff and being interviewed for background information by major newspapers and news shows.

Nanette was anxious to move, also. Her student teaching experience had not been very pleasant. The thought of spending the rest of her work life with eighth and ninth graders was not an appealing thought. Policy work in the nation's capital excited her more. Her goal was to find an interesting job when Simon started first grade. He'd be entering half-day kindergarten in the fall. When she returned to work the following year, it was at the Brookings Institute where she got to interact with serious policy wonks. As far as her career was concerned, Ithaca had little to offer her in comparison.

Before we could settle in, there was a lot to do. Our first concern was buying a house and the most important factor in that decision was which school district to live in. We needed a school system with enough money to provide aides and special programs. That ruled out a few counties, and left us with a choice between Montgomery County in Maryland and Fairfax County in Virginia. Eventually we decided on Maryland; it was close to our family in New Jersey, had a larger Jewish community, and was nearer to some old friends of ours.

A colleague of mine at Cornell had a former student who worked at the Montgomery County Department of Education. She gave us some background information on schools in the county and special programs. We pored over computer printouts listing test scores, school demographics, and the goals each school administration had for the coming year. One school we ruled out immediately. Their goals were fewer fights and improved relations on the playground. Clearly these had been their problems and they were not the kind of thing Alex could deal with.

We called the coordinator of programs for autistic children – we were astonished that they actually had someone in that position – and tried to narrow the list of acceptable neighborhoods. We chose not to look for housing in a neighborhood that fed into a school with a program for autistic children. Those programs were designed for lower functioning children. We knew that Alex would have serious problems but we felt that the best place for him was mainstreamed in a regular classroom. In a school with an autism program it would be too easy to dump him in a special class if he caused a disruption instead of developing ways to help Alex behave in a way to minimize disruptions. We thought the "aide-as-interpreter" model would work best. In the end, we had about four schools we wanted to live near.

That spring we loaded the boys in the car and headed down to hunt for our new home. Washington is about a six-hour drive from Ithaca. Originally, the thought of buying a house in the DC area had been daunting. Once we decided on Montgomery County, acceptable schools, a price range, and the fact that I wanted to be close to a Metro station, our search became quite manageable.

Alex was six and Simon was four. We feared they wouldn't allow us much time to look at houses. To occupy their attention we gave each of them a task. We bought a tape measure for Alex who was assigned the responsibility of recording the dimensions of all the rooms. He was thrilled. Simon had a notebook for writing down his thoughts. This strategy was less successful because Simon couldn't spell, but he took his job of recording his thoughts very seriously. The entire time we were viewing houses and speaking with our real estate agent, we constantly had to be calling out letters to Simon as he labored to write down such hard-hitting critiques as "Yard is good" or "Big bedrooms".

"Daddy, does 'F' come after 'A' in bathroom?"

It did the way he pronounced it.

Nanette and I hate to shop. We found a house in two days. It was three blocks from one of the schools we selected, less than two miles from a Metro stop, and in a neighborhood filled with children. Candlewood Park, in Derwood, Maryland, could be in the dictionary alongside the definition of suburbia. It is a very pleasant community, although there are no wild blueberry bushes or meadows, and way less than an acre of land per house. But we had come to the realization that we wanted suburbia – restaurants, theaters, and easy access to a major city. The country is romantic; suburbia has Home Depot.

Our new house was significantly more spacious than our place in Ithaca. It had a large playroom and a yard that while small in comparison to our old house, was quite substantial by suburban Maryland standards.

Real estate contract in hand, we called the school district office and informed them that we were coming in May of 1994. We were assigned a Pupil Personnel Worker named Edith. Her job was to guide us into the Montgomery County school system. Edith is a transplanted New Yorker, a friendly and perceptive middle-aged woman with glasses and short hair. After one phone conversation she made it apparent she was on Alex's side. Montgomery County is a huge school district with many more layers of bureaucracy than Ithaca. Having someone who appeared so competent in the role as Alex's advocate made us a bit more relaxed.

"Do you have an IEP yet?" she asked.

"No, we thought maybe we should draw one up down there with Alex's new school."

"By time you get down here and organize a meeting it will be too late to affect personnel decisions, like hiring an aide. Besides, his present school knows him better. They can establish much more appropriate goals. Get your IEP written up in Ithaca but go ahead and set up an ARD meeting down here to implement it."

"An ARD meeting?"

"It stands for Admissions, Review, and Dismissal. You'll have to learn a whole new set of acronyms."

We met with the CSE at Caroline.

"So you guys are moving to DC, huh? Well, good luck. We'll miss Alex."

"We were thinking we should go for the gusto with this IEP. I mean, the Ithaca school district won't have to come through with any additional resources, but by law Montgomery County will be obligated to. What do you say to a full-time aide, speech therapy, and a psychologist?"

"Sure, no problem," they chuckled. "How about two aides?"

We were able to set up an ARD meeting for July 11th. It was a repeat of our initial meeting in Ithaca. Huge table, enough staff to man a cruise ship, and lots of paper passing. We told our story, showed them our IEP, and did our best to explain Alex. By the end of the meeting, we were even more skeptical about the county's autism program. It simply was not geared at an appropriate level for Alex. On the other hand, the principal at Candlewood felt that her school could not handle Alex. We all decided that specialists from the school district would search out other possible placements and we would reconvene at a CARD meeting, that is a Central Admissions, Review, and Dismissal.

In the meantime, our main contact with the district was through Edith. She was the only person in the school system that had personal experience with Alex. She had met with him prior to the ARD meeting and ran him through several tests. As usual his academic prowess impressed her, but what impressed us was the sense of Alex she was able to get from her interactions with him and having watched the video of him in his first grade class.

Edith took to Alex quickly. Ironically, although Alex did not make emotional connections with people at that age, he always wore his emotions on his sleeve, and still does. He doesn't hide anything. If he is relaxed his true nature shines through and he can be very endearing. He is a sweet child without a malicious bone in his body, and with no artifice.

Edith was giving him some test, and he was bopping around the room, being a little difficult and not looking at her. As he zipped past her, he banged into her arm, not hard enough to hurt Edith badly but enough to elicit a little cry of "oh". Alex stopped, turned, put his hand on her arm and looked up at her, concerned that he had hurt her.

"It's OK, Alex," she said.

He immediately turned and started zipping around again. But that little connection melted her heart. It's funny how you can get inside someone in an instant, but Edith mentioned that moment to us several times in years to come.

We were determined to go to the wall in our fight for Alex's placement. We had our IEP and we were going to hold the line. We were a little daunted by the layers of bureaucracy but we wanted the best for our son. To a certain extent we had an ally in the local principal. She was not enthusiastic about having Alex as a student. She made that clear. He would create headaches for her, no doubt, both with teachers and with other parents. But she, too, was on our side as far as fighting for resources was concerned. She wanted him in a special program, but if he did end up at Candlewood, she wanted an aide. In fact, she said she could not take him without one.

After the ARD meeting we heard nothing for awhile. We were growing concerned. Weeks were passing by and nothing seemed to be happening. Edith phoned us on August 5th to let us know the county would be calling but another ten days went by with no word. We were agitated. What good was moving to a school district with lots of resources if we were only going to get lost in the shuffle? By the middle of August we were on the phones trying to set up a meeting. If Alex needed an aide there would be precious little time to hire one. We also started inquiring about lawyers. We made sure that the district knew that we knew who were the best hired guns. They knew full well that if they did not find a suitable placement for Alex – at the very least what was written in his IEP – they were out of compliance with the law and that we could and would sue.

We also visited a child psychiatrist in Georgetown – recommended by Edith – for a variety of reasons. First, to get additional ideas about what kind of placements might be beneficial. Second, to send a further signal to the district that we were serious about our son's education and investigating alternatives, and third, just in case Alex had a poor adjustment and we needed extra help.

The summer went by quickly. In the end, the district said they had no special placement. He would have to go to Candlewood. We met with the school staff on August 25th. School was just around the corner. We told them that, legally, Alex had an aide coming to him. We would not send him to school without one. The principal told us we were right to be forceful. She said she would tell the district she would not take him without an aide. We said she couldn't. It was in his IEP.

Then the word came quickly that Alex would have a full-time aide devoted solely to him. School started the following week. They had not even begun a search for candidates, and the speed at which things were progressing was not encouraging.

By the end of the summer we had unpacked, painted, and bought new furniture. My commute was becoming routine and Nanette had begun searching out the other moms in the neighborhood. School was the big question mark looming before us.

We desperately wanted Alex's aide to be in place right from the start. Transitions are difficult for Alex and first impressions – of both teachers and kids – are important. We had moved all this way in large part to give Alex a new start and more resources. Frustration and doubts about our decision started nagging us.

The last working day before school started came but still there was no aide. Our blood went into a low boil. We didn't want him blowing up the first day of school. We didn't want children thinking he was weird or parents freaking out that they had a problem child in their class. That would only feed the doubts the principal had about whether Alex even belonged at Candlewood.

We went on strike. The first day of school came by and we kept Alex at home. We refused to let him attend school unless the district lived up to their responsibilities. We wouldn't be pushed around.

Simon, though, went off to his first day of kindergarten. He was sad. He missed Eli and his other Ithaca friends. He said that he was sure he would never find any friends in Rockville. He was nervous, too. He didn't think he was ready for kindergarten yet. That was the night he told us that he couldn't go to kindergarten because he couldn't even multiply. He came home from his first day of school in tears.

Comforting Simon, fighting for Alex, trying to pull together data on welfare reform as the legislative effort picked up steam, I felt like one of Simon's little rubber action figures being stretched in every possible direction. Nanette was on the warpath but she started having doubts about our decision to relocate to Maryland.

"I don't know, Dan. Do you think this was the right move? I mean, for Simon it may not have been."

"What do you mean? He'll get over it. It's tough for him…"

"It's not like things are so great for Alex either. And now look at Simon."

We had figured Simon would adjust effortlessly. I was surprised that even after a few months he pined for his pals in Ithaca. Nanette did as well. Only I had a ready-made social life at work.

"Listen, Simon," said Nanette, "I'm in the same boat as you. Most of my friends are in Ithaca, too. But if we work together maybe we can help each other get some new friends. Deal?"

"Deal."

The second day of school ended and Simon trudged home. I was still at work but Nanette was there to greet him. He threw down his things and looked at her bright-eyed.

"Guess what, Mom?"

"What?"

"I made a friend today."

"Really? That's great. What's his name?"

"I don't know but he has an X-man backpack."

Earlier that day the school had called Nanette and told her that they had hired an aide. She'd start the next day. Our burgeoning doubts were put on hold.

The next morning Alex and Simon put their backpacks on and headed out, hand in hand with Nanette, to school. They walked down the hill to the school, pausing at the corner for the fifth-grade safety patrol to give them the go-ahead to cross the street. Simon ran to his class, already beginning to feel a little bit at home. Alex walked into his class, oblivious to the fact that he was three days late and already a bit of a celebrity.

33

New Kid on the Block

⅏

Alex's second grade classroom was large and airy. Several windows lined one wall looking out into an atrium at the center of the school. The desks were arranged neatly in rows, but they took up only a portion of the room. Big tables were set up at the back along with bookcases and cabinets. The teacher's desk was off to the side. Posters covered the walls.

Mrs Bagley, Alex's teacher, was a tall soft-spoken woman with blonde hair, glasses, just a few years away from early retirement. She ran a well-ordered, traditional classroom – structured and calm. As calm as you can be with six and seven-year-olds.

We had met Mrs Bagley briefly at one of our several meetings with school officials. She mostly listened and took notes. Although she was an experienced teacher she had never had any special education training and had no idea what to expect from Alex.

None of the teachers Alex had throughout all of elementary school had training in special education – not even one course. They had to learn by doing. The county presumably supplied in-class training in individual cases, but we saw little evidence of that. On rare occasions people from the district would stop by but their help was negligible. They didn't have the time to get to know Alex on any kind of personal level.

Alex's aide, Sandy Brenner, was young – about twenty years old. She also had no special education training. She was a pleasant young woman – quiet with short, black hair. The first time Sandy or Mrs Bagley met Alex was his first day at school.

The day before Alex arrived, the school counselor had come to Mrs Bagley's class to talk to the other children. He brought a collection of shells.

"Do you see all these shells? What do you notice about them?"

"They come from the beach!"

"They're pretty."

"Yes. Very good," he said, "But are they all the same?"

A chorus of "No's."

"How are they different from each other?"

"Some are big and some are little."

"Some have polka-dots."

"Yes, very good. They're all different, but they are still all seashells and they are all very beautiful. Kind of like kids. Even though all children are different, they each have something special about them."

Alex's classmates were told that a new boy was coming, and that he might seem different, but there were special things about him, too, just like with them.

We learned that some parents had heard an autistic boy would be in the class. They were apprehensive. They didn't want someone siphoning off too much attention from their children. Would he be a behavior problem? Would he be violent? No one ever said anything to us until much later after Alex was widely accepted, but even at the time we knew people were curious and were watching. We felt the eyes over our shoulders.

We knew our principal was unhappy. She made it clear then and for the next couple of years that she felt Alex did not belong in a regular classroom. She was worried about parent and student reaction and any undue difficulties for teachers. She was also worried about the precedent it would set. If Alex were mainstreamed, how many more children would follow? The only thing we agreed with her on was the fight for an aide – the more resources the better for everyone.

Alex's short, thin frame was dressed in shorts and a T-shirt. His fine, blond hair fell about his face. He dragged his backpack behind him with one hand, while he held Nanette's hand with the other. He blithely walked into Mrs Bagley's room. Nanette kissed him and told him to have a good day and then turned to leave. Hope and fear enveloped her. She walked home and waited out the morning for a telephone call from the school that thankfully did not come.

Setting Alex afloat in the world is always unnerving. Especially at that age he seemed so detached and ill equipped to handle the vagaries of life. But there is no other choice. And usually Alex surprises us with his resiliency.

Alex was six years old and small for his age. His hair and clothes were always mussed up. His voice was high-pitched, and he spoke with strange inflections. He had a whiny, singsong voice. He had trouble modulating his volume, as well. When he was excited he was too loud and he was too soft otherwise. His pale eyebrows were alternately furrowed with concern or raised high with excitement.

He was the new kid on the block.

Without an aide, Alex's year would have been a disaster. With one, second grade was better than we ever could have hoped, although it wasn't all roses.

Alex had fits. At first, Mrs Bagley kept track of how many he had during the course of a day. Slowly, she switched to how many per week. How many times, that is, that Sandy had to take him into the hall and calm him down. How many times he was sent to the office or the counselor's room teary-eyed, disturbed over some perceived injustice, some arbitrariness of the world, or just some source of frustration.

Alex was trying to fit the huge, ungainly, inconsistent, complicated, idiosyncratic, overwhelming world into the tight little structure he devised in his head. The choices were to block it out or be frustrated by it.

Sandy was the social interpreter and the crutch he needed. She took her job very seriously and both she and Mrs Bagley developed a rapport with him. Alex relied on Sandy tremendously. He loved Sandy. He didn't realize other children didn't have constant companions helping them but then again, he felt no stigma or shame from it either.

Sandy tried to arrange small social interactions on the playground. She made sure Alex stayed focussed on the task at hand. She was a safety valve for his meltdowns, so they rarely became major league. Alex always knew that someone was there to explain the world to him.

We began to have hope that Alex might some day fit into the regular world. It was a vision that seemed impossible when he was in pre-school.

"All he needs now," I thought, "is one friend. The boy has never had a friend."

34

Such Sensitive Children

❧

The teachers and students at Candlewood provided a safe haven for Alex. The rest of the world was not always so accommodating. A particularly painful incident came from an unexpected source.

In 1995, when Alex was in second grade, we were eager to find him a friend. He almost never got together with other children, and when he did, things never worked out well. He didn't connect with other children. He had a hard time finding activities they could do together. Pretend play was beyond him and many of the board games he liked were too advanced for his peers. He lacked any negotiating skills and at the first sign of conflict or disagreement he would decide to go it alone and ignore the other child. A few times when we did have a little boy over our house, we ended up playing with him while Alex was off on the computer. We felt bad for his guest who had been left in the lurch.

Still, when someone did play a game with Alex – usually an adult or a much older child – Alex was thrilled. He would laugh and bounce around the room with excitement. He didn't know who people were but somehow he enjoyed the idea of doing things with them. Even nowadays, he will hug people who express an interest and enthusiasm for math, or try to tickle them. He'll ask any adult who comes over our house if they want to play a game or answer a math question. This pleases and puzzles us. What is it about Alex that makes people both important and irrelevant to him at the same time?

Anyway, we decided to make a concerted effort to find Alex a friend. Somewhere out there, we thought, a child like Alex exists, a child he can bond with. We heard about special classes that the Johns Hopkins University offered for gifted children. Maybe, we thought, he could meet a nerdy kid who likes to play games and do math. We called them up but unfortunately their classes didn't begin until third grade. They told us of another group that organized classes and social activities for profoundly gifted children.

"Hello, my name is Daniel Mont. Some people at Johns Hopkins told me about your group. My son, Alex, is seven years old and is very bright. We thought it might be a good place for him to find friends. Can you tell me more about the kind of things you do?"

"Well, we offer classes and activities in a wide range of academic areas," said the woman who coordinated the program and who also had a child in the group. "In addition, we serve as a support group and social outlet for profoundly gifted children. We find they have special needs and really need to be in their own group to flourish."

"That sounds great."

"I have to tell you, though, that only children with an IQ of 150 or over are allowed to join."

Bells went off in my head. Something didn't feel right but what she said next made me feel better.

"I know that sounds élitist or something, but we decided to do that after we had some problems with pushy parents. We felt we need to keep out children who were being pushed to achieve. There are lots of bright, normally gifted children whose parents are out there looking for enrichment activities. But our group is profoundly gifted. These children are truly beyond normally gifted children. They learn differently and have different problems. A lot of them are social outcasts. They're misunderstood. They need a place to be with children like themselves."

My heart almost skipped a beat. Profoundly gifted. Social misfits. Need to find children like themselves. Maybe this was a place for Alex to find peers. Who knew? Maybe some of the other children were autistic.

"I need to tell you that Alex is high-functioning autistic…"

"What do you mean by that?"

I explained. She said his idiosyncrasies and skills sounded an awful lot like the children in their group. We were thrilled.

We took Alex to a psychologist they recommended to get his IQ tested. We were nervous because studies we read claimed that autistic children tend to score lower on the type of IQ test she used because it was a verbally oriented test. We drove up to Baltimore, hoping Alex would score high enough. It was odd to look in the back seat at my little seven-year-old and think that a standardized test might make a big difference in his life.

Simon and Nanette went out for donuts while I accompanied Alex up to the psychologist's office. She let me sit across from them during the test. She and Alex shared a couch. My nerves were on edge. I leaned forward on my seat with every question. Each time he got something correct I wanted to shout. Each time he missed something my chest contracted. A couple of times I thought he didn't get an answer because of language issues. I had to fight to restrain my compulsion to yell out, "Wait! If you let me explain the question, I know he could get it right."

The test ended. By this time, Simon and Nanette were in the waiting room. The psychologist sent Alex out to be with them. Nanette wanted to come in and hear the results with me but the psychologist only wanted the parent who had seen the test in the room. We were a little put off by this, but since this was a one-time visit we acquiesced.

"Did he pass? Did he score over 150? You see, I read that autistic children sometimes don't do as well on this type of test because…"

"Relax. He scored over 150."

"Thank God." I started to cry. "I don't care if he scored 151 or 201, I just want him to get in this group so maybe he could meet a friend."

She passed me a box of tissues. I thanked her and headed out to the waiting room to give Nanette the good news. The next step was that month's meeting of the group. I called the coordinator to tell her that Alex passed the test and that we were coming. She was pleased.

A few weeks later we drove up to Baltimore to Towson State College where they had their meetings. We were running late so we grabbed a bite at a Kentucky Fried Chicken that by the end of the evening had Nanette's and my digestive tracts in knots. The meeting took place in a large classroom in a fairly nondescript building. The other parents greeted us warmly. The kids were sent into the next room with a babysitter.

The parents settled in around a table and the coordinator passed out some reading material. As I started leafing through it, I glanced up at Nanette. I could see her reaction was similar to mine – revulsion. The first article was touting a recently published book called *The Bell Curve** as one of the most important pieces of research ever. That book, written by Herrnstein and Murray, made the case for how important IQ was and how fantastic it was at predicting future success. The book goes on to claim that genetic differences in IQ can explain the earnings gap between blacks and whites. I had read several scathing reviews of this book and although I admit I never read it myself, I had attended several lectures by economists I respect pointing out the methodological problems in the book. Just that week I had heard a radio interview with Stephen Jay Gould, a noted author and paleontologist, explaining how this was another chapter in a long history of people using pseudo-scientific means to explain racial superiority.

Again, I had not read the book myself so I couldn't automatically dismiss it although I was highly suspicious. It was very unsettling to be with a group of people who were so willing to embrace it, without any questioning.

The other items in the reading packet were not consoling. They basically reveled in how wonderful children with high IQs were. One article claimed these children were especially sensitive to the needs of other children – how much more sophisticated they were than "normal" children. That clearly has not been my experience, and as I interacted

---

*   Herrnstein, R. and Murray, C. (1994) *The Bell Curve.* New York: The Free Press

with those children, my impression was that their parents for the most part were raising arrogant little people. These children were bright, no doubt about it. They were profoundly gifted. But I had known children like that in Ithaca. Every year some professor's kid at Cornell was wowing people at the university while he was a pre-teen. The difference with these children, I hate to say, is that their parents weren't that bright. Our discussion of IQ tests, statistics, and the education system that night made that immediately apparent. Nanette and I quickly backed off during the discussion because we didn't want to make waves. But the problem, as we saw it, was that these parents were in awe of their children. They were making them feel like they were better than "normal" people. Not smarter (in terms of the type of intelligence IQ tests measure) but better.

Near the end of the meeting, Simon came into the room. He had wet his pants. He was five years old and had not done that for a long time. He also seemed very down. We went with him into the other room. The other children had been ignoring him. You see, some of the siblings in the room were members of the group. Others were just siblings and not worthy of attention, as far as the other children were concerned. Simon had been writing numbers on the board and trying to add them. That's what Alex did. Simon was trying to show how smart he was. I felt sick. Nanette almost cried. Both of our blood pressures rose. We vowed then and there that Simon was never coming back to that group.

"I can't believe we did that to Simon," said Nanette.

"It's only one time. We'll never bring him back."

"Simon never *ever* adds up numbers like that. The poor boy. Did you see his face?"

We left that evening in a quandary. We knew that we had to keep Simon away from that scene. We also had no desire to associate with most of those parents, ourselves. But we had met one very nice woman whose child seemed as gifted as Alex was mathematically and also as in love with games. Maybe, just maybe, this little boy, who was about Alex's age, could be a friend. We were resolved to give it a try. We would sign him up for a course and try to get together with this little boy. As it turns out, that was not an option.

"Hello, Mr Mont?"

"Yes?"

"Hi, I'm glad you're in. I wanted to tell you how nice it was to meet you last night."

"Thanks. I'm glad we were able to make it to your meeting. We're looking forward to signing Alex up for one of your classes."

"Well...that's what I want to talk to you about. I'm so sorry. But after the meeting the other children, felt that Alex was a little odd. That he didn't really belong in the group. You know our group is for a very special kind of child and these children can usually tell right away if a new kid belongs, and we always trust their judgement. Maybe he didn't fit in because he is autistic."

"You mean, you're not letting Alex join?" I was incredulous. "He passed your IQ test."

"Yes, but the other children feel he really isn't one of them. Do you know what I mean? I'm sure there are other programs he can sign up for. We're sorry, we feel bad because you and Nanette were so nice."

"Well, what did he do?" I fought to restrain my anger.

"I'm sorry, Mr Mont. Our decision is final. We really have to trust our children on this."

I hung up the phone. I was furious. Absolutely furious. What kind of monsters were these people raising, anyway? "They are not like us. We can tell if he belongs."

I wrote as scathing a letter to them as I could. I wanted my points to get through so I rewrote the letter a few times to make sure I didn't sound like I was ranting.

I am very saddened and disappointed that you have rejected Alex, not because I feel this is a missed opportunity for him to learn more academically. He will continue to learn math and science with as much glee and at the same rate as your children. I am saddened and angered by the unfeeling way in which he was treated. You claim that your children are more sensitive than other children are – that they do not fit in socially and have experienced rejection. How, then, can they turn around and inflict the same thing on another child because he is odd?

You didn't talk to us about Alex's behavior. You didn't suggest we attend classes or hire an aide – which we probably would have been willing to do. You didn't talk to his teachers to see how he fits into a mainstreamed class at school. You put forth absolutely no effort in trying to help a child who has some of the same problems as your own children.

You could have taken this as an opportunity to teach your own children about compassion, or community, or even human development. You could have structured a class around developmental issues so your children could learn about how the brain functions so they could be more understanding of people. You could have at least talked with us to see what options existed. Alex passed your entry exam. As you explained to me over the phone, that was the condition for joining your group.

You should be aware that we could sue you under the Americans with Disability Act. You use public facilities and are not legally allowed to exclude Alex. We do not plan to do so, however. In this life, you have to pick your battles, and since we primarily saw your group as a way for Alex to meet friends, we don't feel you are worth the trouble. Maybe in the future, you could use opportunities such as Alex to teach your children that there are things of value other than high IQs, such as a caring and open heart.

We sent the letter. Each day I checked the answering machine and the mail. I wanted them to feel bad. I wanted to wring their necks. I wanted either an abject apology or a fight.

We never heard back.

35

A Blessing

∞

Alex's reception was much better among the children of Candlewood. In fact, given the way Alex treated them, at times I was surprised at how nice they were to him. Alex had no understanding of social niceties.

"Do you want to play this with me, Alex?"

"NO! I don't want to play with you, so go away."

"Are you sure, Alex?"

"I said, 'no'. Go away. Why is this person bothering me?"

Mrs Bagley told us once that a child ended up in tears. But still, they were nice to him – even though he had no idea who they were. One boy, named John, particularly took Alex under his wing, which was great for Alex since John was one of the more liked and respected members of the class. He even invited Alex to his birthday party. Alex was very excited. By this time in the year Simon had been to many parties, sometimes two on a weekend. Alex was not invited to parties. He was thrilled that it was now his turn, especially since the party was taking place at a Washington Warthogs game. The Warthogs are an indoor soccer team, and they offered party deals that included cake in a special room, some soccer activities, and then tickets to the game. Of course, I couldn't send Alex by himself like the other parents did. I accompanied him. He had a great time, but I had mixed feelings. Alex didn't interact with the other boys.

When I asked him if they were in his class – which I knew they were – he responded that he was not sure.

Looking at the other boys, it was clear that they were pals. They joked around. They were a gang. Alex sat with me, apart from the action. He clutched his party favors and watched the game – keenly interested in the penalties, the game clock, and the various rules. He had a great time but it was difficult for me to understand what he got out of the event that would have been different than just going with me. But it was different. This was a birthday party and for some reason unfathomable to me, that was important.

It is a minor miracle to me that Alex has barely been teased or ridiculed by his classmates – not at the Special Children's Center and not throughout elementary school. Why haven't children teased him? The answer is difficult to pin down. Children are notorious for being cruel and ostracizing children who are different from the "norm." Maybe as Alex moves on into adolescence his good fortune will change. I certainly hope not. But I think the secret to Alex's being accepted is multifaceted. First, Alex is innocent, sweet, and totally honest and straightforward. What you see is what you get. He is incapable of subterfuge. He doesn't understand it, and he sincerely wishes ill on no one. Second, his brilliance in academic subjects has bought him a level of acceptance. When Alex has acted strange or has had tantrums or has demonstrated a complete lack of understanding of what other children consider the simplest things, they have not been able to dismiss him as just being stupid or odd. They know he is a genius. He demonstrates his intellectual acumen on a daily basis. Therefore, when he acts like a child half his age or is incapable of joining in with others, it is apparent to his classmates that this behavior is a reflection of his disability. That buys him acceptance and makes children pause and try to understand him. Finally, Alex lacks arrogance. Children are not threatened or annoyed by his aptitude because he doesn't think of himself as superior, and they don't feel inferior because it is clear that his gifts are accompanied by problems and difficulties they would not wish to have.

Sometimes his social problems turn into an advantage. When he was in second grade, a little girl named Emily approached Nanette while she was chaperoning a field trip.

"I like Alex because he is so modern."

"Modern?" asked Nanette, somewhat puzzled.

"Yes. He doesn't tease the girls like all the other boys."

Nanette didn't have the heart to tell her that Alex would have been hard pressed to identify which children were girls and which were boys. But, in a way, being oblivious to gender is modern, I suppose.

By the end of the year, Mrs Bagley told us that she thought having Alex in her class was a blessing.

"What do you mean by that?" I asked.

"Well, Alex makes you look at everything in a new way. You have to question everything you do."

This touched me deeply. Mrs Bagley was nearing retirement. She was a committed teacher, but I had noticed that many of her worksheets were dated several years earlier. It's easy in any job you've done for years to be on automatic pilot. But even at that point in her career Alex had made the world new for her again

36

Stamping Out Ambiguity

ೞ

"Mrs Stocklin! Mrs Stocklin! It is 9:17 and the schedule says math starts at 9:15."

As Alex entered third grade in the fall of 1995, he had become much more able to express himself. He was assigned to Mrs Stocklin's class. Joanne's classroom was a little more laid back than Mrs Bagley's was. She was younger, with long blonde hair usually kept up in a loose bun. She was very affectionate with Alex and he often climbed up in her lap.

Alex started enjoying school more, as well, as the work became a little more academic. Most subjects were very easy for him, but there was enough meat in some of the assignments that with a little fiddling he could turn a simple problem into a complex one and entertain himself.

He was still a stickler for rules and punctuality, though. Mrs Stocklin eventually had to remove any mention of time from her daily schedule or Alex would be on her back if she wasn't super-punctual. The difference we began observing, though, was that as he got older he found people's deviations from schedules and rules funny instead of disconcerting. As a matter of fact, when his response to such situations moved more towards the panic and anger of previous days, it was a pretty clear indicator that there was some other source of stress in his life.

But even if he was in a good mood he could never let an ambiguity go unchecked. He would interrupt Mrs Stocklin whenever she was explaining any math or science concept if she wasn't doing it correctly. Even if she was technically correct, he would often run up to the board to explain how she could solve a problem more efficiently or in a more general fashion.

"And when he explains something mathematical at the board," said Mrs Stocklin, "he does it beautifully. He doesn't stutter or do start, stop, and then re-start his sentences. He doesn't struggle at all. He draws charts and graphs and lays everything out in a very logical way."

The only breakdown in communication occurred if he was correcting what he considered a silly mistake. Then, he would laugh hysterically. So hard, in fact, that he couldn't even sit on his chair.

But God forbid if an ambiguity showed up on a test. Alex has taken many tests, not just at school but standardized tests aimed at assessing his math ability and also tests administered to special needs children to isolate their problems. Time and again, he finds ambiguous questions. When he does, he can enter meltdown mode again. Scores are very important to him and if he thinks the grading is unfair he considers it the ultimate injustice.

In fourth grade he participated in the National Math Olympiad. The Math Olympiad consists of five tests with five questions each. A very, very small percentage of children – especially fourth graders – get a perfect score. Alex had 20 out of 20 going into the last test. He very much wanted to ace it.

The last test had this question: You have a pool that is 12 feet wide and 20 feet long. If you want to build a walkway around the pool with two-foot square tiles, how many tiles do you need? The trick to the question was not forgetting about the corners.

This question quickly reduced Alex to tears.

"How do you know how wide the walkway is supposed to be?"

The test writers just assumed you would know they meant a two-foot wide walkway because that's how wide the tiles were, but they never said that explicitly. Alex went up to his fourth grade teacher, Ms Cavanaugh, who was proctoring the exam. He wanted to know how wide the walkway was supposed to be. Obviously she couldn't tell him. She had to take him into the hall to quiet him down. He was full of anxiety and the clock was ticking.

"How wide do you think the walkway is, Alex?"

"Is it supposed to be two-feet wide?"

"What do you think?"

"I DON'T KNOW!"

"If that's what you think, then go ahead and assume that."

"But I can't be sure."

"If it's not right, Alex, we can write a protest letter to the test writers."

Alex went back in and aced the test. Later that year he had to fill out a questionnaire that asked him what he wanted to be when he grew up. He replied, "A math test question editor." That's my son. At age nine he had a mission in life – to stamp out test writing ambiguity.

His sense of exactness comes through in everything. I read a newspaper story on prosecuting children as adults for certain crimes. In the article, the reporter presented a moral reasoning test that children under seven fail. I decided to give it to Alex and Simon.

"OK guys. Say John broke one mug when he threw it at his sister, but Sally broke six mugs while trying to help her dad load the dishwasher. Who did the worse thing?"

Simon immediately said, "John, because he was doing something wrong. Sally accidentally broke the mugs while she was trying to be helpful."

According to the article, Simon answered the question correctly. Children under seven, however, often say Sally did the worse thing because she broke more mugs.

"It depends," said Alex. "Why did John throw the mug?"

"I don't know, Alex, maybe because his sister was annoying him or because he was being mean or just trying to be funny in a reckless way."

"What if his sister was trying to kill him?"

"Hmmm," I said. "I guess you're right, Alex. Technically, the answer is ambiguous. But in the vast majority of cases, little brothers and sisters don't act like that."

"Well, how do you know that in THIS case?"

The test writer was making assumptions. Alex doesn't. The assumptions were reasonable and would probably be made by most people without even thinking about them, but Alex doesn't take much for granted.

And he never lied, or tried to brown-nose a teacher.

"Alex always told it like it was," said Mrs Stocklin. "And when he was happy, I was so happy because I knew that he was really, really happy. If he liked something or hugged me I knew it was completely genuine."

37

Going Hazy

C3

My mother's condition grew worse. The laser surgery did not work and it soon became apparent to everyone that she was going blind, but no one would admit it.

"If I can't see, what's the point in living?"

She bought a large-screen television and positioned her chair three feet in front of it. The world was going hazy but my mom was convinced that with one more operation she would be able to see. After several, there was no real hope for improvement.

Debbie and I hooked her up with some organizations for the blind in New Jersey. She bought some optical equipment at home so that she could read and started attending training sessions to become a counselor for elderly people with vision problems.

The diabetes, though, kept eating away at her. She started having kidney problems; her body filled with fluid and her joints ached. She developed neuropathy in her hands and feet, and her lack of mobility added to her weight problems. The doctors told her that she was developing almost every complication diabetes could cause.

She became too weak to travel. Besides, she couldn't see what she would be travelling to. Her eyes became too bad to play Mah Jong, and she started losing touch with her friends. She continued to volunteer for a couple of clubs but it was usually doing things like bookkeeping and arranging events. They were mostly solitary activities. She planned events that she sometimes couldn't even attend. Even her counseling was done over the phone. Except for my father she was basically alone. The days were huge unfillable blocks of time.

She still tried to sound optimistic but her façade was beginning to crack. For the first time my mom started showing her fear and the extent to which her medical problems affected her. She tried not to, but her strength started to fail her. Then one day she was rushed to the hospital with congestive heart failure. She recovered – and with no significant damage to her heart – but it made it clear how serious her condition was. My parents decided to move down to Leisure World, a retirement community six miles from where we lived.

"There's more to do there," said my father. "There's even a bus that can take Mom to the Clubhouse or to the shopping center. And, that way you'll be near us in case we need help."

Debbie was living in England and while Diane was doing a lot better – living on her own and holding down a series of temporary jobs – she wasn't as stable as me and Nanette. Shortly afterward she followed my parents to the DC area.

"This way I'll really get to know your children," my mother said.

"And we'll be close to the Johns Hopkins hospital," said my dad.

"Right. Maybe those bright young doctors can fix me up."

38

Learning to Cope

❧

Alex's progress was sure but slow. Sometimes we felt as if we were treading water. Alex's curriculum was different from other children's, at least in emphasis. His major tasks were keeping his things organized, saying hello to people and responding to them, recognizing people, keeping his voice at the proper volume, learning to be part of a group, and sharing things and playing games with other children. Academics were secondary.

Nancy, his speech therapist, was the main constant throughout Alex's elementary school years. She was very straightforward and always willing to talk about Alex, counsel Nanette when there were problems, and search out new ideas. One of her main activities during Alex's first year at Candlewood was roaming the halls with Alex and saying hello to passers-by.

"Alex, here comes Mr Smith. Say, 'Hello, how are you?'"

In a singsong voice that exaggerated the rhythms of normal speech, Alex would say, "Hello. How are you?"

"Why, fine, Alex, and how are you?"

"Fine."

"Remember to look at Mr Smith when you're talking to him."

Alex's eyes would lock on those of the other person unblinking, with an unnatural intensity, his chin pushed forward. In a loud, clipped voice he would say, "Fine!"

Nancy also worked with Mrs Bagley and Mrs Stocklin in devising behavior modification systems to encourage Alex to achieve certain goals. Behavior modification has always worked well with Alex because of his love for systems and earning points. When he was still in kindergarten and first grade he would never stay focussed on getting dressed in the morning. We had many struggles and tried many strategies. The one that finally worked was "10 points in 10 minutes." We assigned each article of clothing a point value. Two points for his shirt, two points for his shorts, two for his underwear, and one each for his socks and shoes. His goal was to get ten points in ten minutes. A perfect score meant that he was completely dressed. When I told this to a co-worker she asked what he received for his points. Could he, for example, buy a toy with 100 points?

"No. He just gets the points."

"Only points?" she asked quizzically.

"He loves points."

At school, he received points for putting his backpack away, hanging up his coat, saying hello, and any number of things. At home we had point systems for interacting with Simon and clearing the table. Simon requested that he have a way of earning points as well and we obviously obliged. Life was a constant tallying of behaviors. Once Simon was involved, however, the points quickly became a way to earn treats. Points for points' sake were not compelling enough. The goal was to add new point-gathering activities and drop old ones as they became second nature.

Eventually their ways of earning points became more abstract. Ten points were awarded if we could go a whole day without any fights between Alex and Simon. Each time we intervened they lost a point. Alex was unhappy with this system because his point-earning ability was not solely under his control. We had many heated discussions about that and to this day he is uneasy with any type of group-based award. At school he gets upset when prizes are awarded to the best-behaved table or if all the children are denied playground privileges because they are being too rowdy. He views this as patently unfair, and can get extremely agitated. But the world isn't always fair or totally under your control. That is one of the most important lessons that Alex has yet to learn.

As Alex moved into third grade, his ability to cope with the classroom was substantially improved. We still felt he needed an aide, however, and were thrilled when Sandy was re hired.

As Alex's ability to function improved, his relationship with Sandy became more tense. He started to resent having her around. Sandy took her job very seriously. She was always looking for ways to help Alex and was constantly trying to keep him focussed, or improve his behavior.

There is an inherent problem with special education aides. The goal of an aide like Sandy is to work herself out of a job. We wanted her to do as little as possible to keep Alex on track and well behaved – to help him become more self-sufficient. If he could survive a day with no assistance from Sandy, then so much the better. But from Sandy's point of view that meant she was useless. We disagreed. She was there as a safety valve and another pair of eyes to help us know what was going on in Alex's life. If Alex could make it on his own, then she could just help out in the classroom as a general aide, we thought.

Sandy felt that she had to be doing something with Alex. And face it, with any child there are always things to work on and room for improvement. As Joanne told us, Sandy started holding Alex to a higher standard than the other children, even though Joanne tried to explain to her that she needed to ease up. Joanne told us she thought Sandy was placing higher demands on him than the other children faced.

"Sit up straight."

"Pay attention."

"Are you doing your work, or are you daydreaming?"

"Now, be neat!"

Being nudged like that would drive anyone batty. Alex started getting annoyed with Sandy. While he loved her in second grade, he resented her in third grade.

Nanette and Joanne told Sandy to ease up, but she found it difficult. She genuinely cared for Alex and wanted to be more proactive. Like most aides, she felt that if she wasn't "doing something", she wasn't earning her keep. Once she was called out of the room for most of the day to help deal with another difficult child. When she returned, she asked Joanne if Alex had been all right. Joanne replied that he had done fine. No problem. She said Sandy almost seemed disappointed.

Alex needed Sandy, but not continually, only sporadically. He still had meltdowns and was still confused at times, but he was becoming more accustomed to the NT world and was closer to going it on his own.

When fourth grade rolled around we all decided to ratchet down Alex's aide time. He only had an aide to help him get settled at the beginning of the day and help him get ready to leave at the end. Alex's fourth grade teacher, Ms. Cavanaugh, was filled with lots of energy, and showered the kids with love. She, too, understood our conundrum. Alex disliked aides, and they seemed to put too high demands on him, but without them he would be an organizational mess.

39

Black History Month

CB

Alex, like many autistic people, often does not understand the ways of the NT. Sometimes, though, his lack of understanding demonstrates more about the deficiencies of NTs than autistic people.

For the past few years, February has been a month filled with disbelief and incredulity. February is Black History Month and Alex just doesn't get it. In fourth grade he had to do a report on a famous African-American. He picked Jackie Robinson.

"Hey, Alex, how's that report coming?"

"OK. I'm almost finished."

"Great."

"I have a question."

"What, Alex?"

"Jackie Robinson was a great player, right? Why didn't people want him on their team?"

"Because he was black." I scanned Alex's half-written report. It was filled with statistics demonstrating what a great player Robinson was.

"But he would help them win games, right?"

"Right."

"So why wouldn't they want him?"

He innocently looked up at me. He had a little smile on his face. He was expecting a clever answer, like a secret solution to a puzzle.

"Because he was black, Alex. And lots of white people either hated blacks or didn't want anything to do with them."

"But why? He was a great player, right?"

"They knew he'd help them win more games, but they didn't think it was worth it because then they'd have to associate with blacks. They'd also have to admit that blacks were as good as whites."

"But black people are as good as white people, right?"

"Of course."

"So why wouldn't they want him on their team?"

How do you explain racism to someone who lives by logic? How do you explain it to someone who honestly, completely cannot relate to judging people by the color of their skin?

I like to think of myself as non-racist, but I was raised in this society. When I pass a group of not very well-dressed black youths on the street I react differently than if they were white. I don't like that about myself but I can't help it. Sometimes I catch myself pre-judging people because of their ethnicity. When I am conscious of what I'm doing, I back off, but it can be a reflex. Alex doesn't have that reflex. It's an NT thing. I almost don't want to explain it to him.

"You see, Alex, sometimes it is out of ignorance. Or people like to feel better about themselves so they put others down to make them think that they are the best. Or maybe they feel that way because they learned it from their parents when they were kids and never got over it."

Alex looks at me with total incomprehension. It makes no sense, and I agree.

Women's Studies is equally confusing.

"Daddy, if the wife of the president is called the first lady, what is the husband of the president called?"

"Well, Alex, there never has been a woman president."

"REALLY? That's surprising." His eyes are opened wide. "Why?"

When he learned that women did not have the right to vote until the twentieth century I think he just gave up trying to understand.

Other things that are less profound also confuse him.

"Alex, your shirt is on backwards."

"I know."

"Turn it around."

"Why?"

"Because it is on backwards."

"It feels OK."

"Yes, but it looks funny. It belongs the other way."

Of course, sometimes convention must be obeyed. Alex has no sense of modesty. He would walk buck naked through Grand Central Station. We'd be sitting in a restaurant and he would get up to use the bathroom. Alex, even at ten years old, would start undressing himself along the way. He'd emerge outside "au natural" when we were chatting with neighbors.

Drumming in the rule about not displaying your private parts in public took quite some time. He still does not understand why this is such a big deal, but thankfully it is one rule he has come close to mastering.

Alex will often unintentionally point out the foibles of the NT mind. In fifth grade, advertising amused him no end.

"I can understand commercials for cars that tell you the cost of the car and the gas mileage, but what is this one about?"

"Well, Alex, the company is trying to create an image for their car. They are trying to make people think it is a cool car to drive."

"An IMAGE? What do you mean?"

"Like, here is this beautiful woman driving this car past these magnificent mountains. If you drive this car, you'll feel like you are beautiful and driving through the mountains."

"What if you don't live near mountains?"

"That's not the point. I mean...well...like...cool people drive this car so if you drive this car you'll feel cool, too."

"I would want a car with good gas mileage."

Simon will leap for the newest pop culture fad. In fact, he is often so attuned to these things that he is ahead of the curve. Not Alex.

"Why would you pay $100 for a beanie baby when you could buy another one for $5?"

I try to explain. I even ended up giving him a history lesson about speculative markets and bubble economies. Tulips in Holland. Land deals in the South Pacific. The stock market crash of 1929. There are many examples throughout history of NTs flying off half-crazed by the pursuit of value that only exists because others think it exist, and as soon as they don't...poof!

Alex is a comparison shopper extraordinaire. He buys generic.

I think Alex thinks NTs are nuts, and sometimes, I have to go along with him. There's an organization called CAN – Cure Autism Now. Needless to say, it doesn't have many fans among the autistic people I know. Instead, the autistic people's organization printed up their own T-shirt, Cure All Neurologically Typicals – CANT.

40

Mr Hustle

CR

"Guess what, Dad?" said Simon. "Alex came into our class today."
"Wait until you hear this," said Nanette, getting dinner ready in the kitchen. I threw my briefcase down and picked up the mail as I walked over to Simon who was doing his homework on the dining room table. He was in second grade and had Mrs Bagley as a teacher – the same teacher his brother had had. As it happened, Alex was in the classroom next door.

Simon was the teacher's pet. He genuinely strived to please his teachers. He was well behaved and an eager learner. He did really well in school and could get turned on by just about anything. He also had a penchant for talking. Once, when he was in preschool, he dominated circle time day after day with impromptu stories. His favorite was an ever-changing and ever-lengthening rendition of Jack and the Beanstalk. His teachers told us that once he was on a roll he was almost unstoppable.

"Mrs Bagley didn't know the answer to a question, so she went next door to get Alex."

"She brought him into the classroom?"

"Yep."

"Did he know the answer?"

Simon gave me an exaggerated roll of his eyes and put his pencil down. "Of course, Dad. What did you think?"

"What was the question?"

"How do you convert degrees Fahrenheit to degrees Celsius."

"And she brought him right into the class?"

"Yes. Everybody said, 'your brother is so smart!'"

I scanned Simon's face looking to see if he was proud or resentful.

"I wonder where he learned the formula," I said.

"He knows *everything.* I wish I was that smart."

"You are plenty smart."

"Dad, you don't have to say all that again."

"But it's true!" Chagrined I went into the kitchen to help Nanette. Simon went back to his homework.

Doing things with Simon was a joy because everything was so easy. Homework wasn't a big deal. Socializing wasn't a big deal. Life with him was relaxing.

"If raising normal kids is like this," I said to Nanette, "why do people complain it's hard work?"

Around this time Simon wanted to start playing soccer. We signed him up for a team and I agreed to be the assistant coach. We headed off for Candlewood for the first practice. The children on the team ran around like maniacs, following the ball like a herd of wild animals. There was little sense or reason to their actions other than an intense desire to be the one who kicked the ball. They were having a blast. The sun had dipped below the horizon and a breeze blew over the open field next to the school. The weather was perfect. The setting was perfect. I stood on the sidelines and chattered with the other parents as the head coach shouted encouragement. I felt free. I was actually able to talk to the other parents and not worry.

The ball was kicked to an open area of the field and Simon was the first to get to it. He took possession of the ball and turned to start heading the other direction. As he turned about four other children started rushing toward him. They barely brushed him but he was overwhelmed and fell to the ground. He burst into tears.

"It's OK, Simon. You didn't get hit that hard. You're all right."

He continued sobbing. It must have been scary but I couldn't see why he couldn't brush it off, since he didn't really get hurt. All the other children were getting knocked down the same way and getting up like it was nothing. I tried not to show my annoyance.

"Do you want to sit out for a minute and then go back in?"

He shook his head no and kept crying. I saw the other coach look over at me. I thought, "Don't be such a cry baby. Damn it! Now this is going to be a big deal, too?" I tried to calm Simon down. I tried not to say those things but I must have shown them. I was embarrassed that the thoughts even came into my head, but they were there. Across the field, the other children were playing. Their parents were talking, and here I was again with a crying child. "It's not fair!" I thought. "This one's not supposed to give me problems like this."

"I don't want to play soccer anymore," he said in between big, gasping breaths.

"You mean, tonight?"

"Ever."

"Come on! You got knocked down. All the kids get knocked down."

"I'm sorry! I'm not them!"

I felt like an ass. I also wanted him back on that field. Why? So he would learn to be tough and not give up so easily? So I could for once in my life have the same experience as other parents? Who was acting more like a baby, him or me?

Simon went on and played again and has played one or two sports every season, and gone to soccer and basketball camps. He's small but he gives everything he has. He's Mr Hustle. His size and his effort on the court combine to send him reeling to the floor several times a game. He still cries more easily than most kids, but he picks himself up and plays on. His baby face transforms into a look of dogged determination. When he decides to do something he goes all out. He throws himself in front of oncoming attackers. He lunges for balls. Sometimes he cries out of frustration or the intensity of his effort. It's the last few minutes of a basketball game and he is dribbling down the court and the ball gets stolen; or, he penetrates into the lane but there is no one there to dish off to. You can see the veins in his neck. You would think it's a matter of life or death.

He tries for a steal but ends up on the floor, called for a foul. I can see he is on the verge of tears.

"What's wrong?"

"I...DON'T ...KNOW."

"Settle down, guy. Take a seat."

"I want to play."

"Simon, if you get hurt and cry, that's OK. But don't cry because things aren't going the way you want. If you cry it means you are hurt bad enough to sit down for awhile."

I'm confused. I don't want to tell my boy not to cry. Lots of boys have gotten messed up with that advice. On the other hand, he needs to let things roll off his back – be able to try hard but keep perspective.

"I want to go back in."

"OK. Next time out."

I'm Simon's basketball coach. One thing I can always rely on from him is 100 per cent effort. Sometimes I wonder where he gets that kind of intensity. Nanette and I sure don't have it.

When the game is over, Simon shrugs off the loss and moves on to the next event. By the end of the day he is exhausted. After the requisite goading, he climbs into bed and Nanette or I read him a few chapters from one of the books we're working on and then turn out the light.

41

Front Page News

 C3

When I start talking about my children, I can't stop. My friends at work know this. I often pop into their offices with a story or a problem or a boast. I usually have to restrain myself to not talk too much. Sometimes I fail.

As the Math Olympiad progressed in fourth grade, I kept a few friends at work informed of Alex's scores. At first I was light-hearted about it, but as he aced each successive exam I became more nervous. By the last one I was on the edge of my seat waiting for the final score. Part of me just wanted him to do well like any father would, but part of me is always looking for validation that he really is that exceptional in math because it will make his life so much easier, his "oddities" that much more accepted.

Nanette and I projected a low-key attitude about it at home. It would be stupid to put pressure on Alex for something like this. We didn't want him to feel any worse than he would anyway if he missed a question, and we didn't want Simon to have to listen to discussions about Alex's quest for a perfect score.

The afternoon of the last installment I had a hard time focussing at work, wondering about how the exam went. The phone rang. It was Nanette with the good news. He aced it. I was elated. She told me the story of the ambiguous question and Alex's concern over making the wrong assumption. For the first time I became aware that this was important to him, too. He never mentioned it.

Unable to contain my excitement, I wandered across the hall to a couple of my friends' offices and gave them the full lowdown. They had been following along and rooting for Alex, as well.

"You know," said Susan, a computer programmer in my division, "I've been telling my neighbor some of your Alex stories. She's a *Washington Post* reporter and she said if you are interested, they'd probably write a story about Alex, especially now that he got this perfect score."

Nanette and I were uncertain. We talked it over for weeks. Our initial reaction was excitement and pride. Basically, we thought it would be incredibly cool to see Alex's picture in the paper. Then, we hesitated. We didn't know if Alex would like the publicity. Were we exploiting him just so we could have a "proud parent" moment? And how would Simon react? On the other hand, Nanette and I greedily ate up stories about parents and their autistic children that appeared in the press. Recently, *USA Today* had run a story about an autistic teenager who was a member of his school's wrestling team. Reading about his teammate's acceptance of him gave me a lot of hope for Alex's adolescence. And then there had been the books we read when Alex was diagnosed. They had been a source of great solace.

We decided to put the question to Alex. "Alex," we asked, "the newspaper wants to write a story about your perfect score. They'll mention that you are autistic. Do you want them to do it?"

"Yes!"

That answered that. Simon agreed. Alex was very proud of his accomplishment and for the first time he began to have an inkling that he had a special talent.

I told my friend Susan that we would meet with the reporter from the *Post*. She told her neighbor who relayed the message to the Montgomery County office of the paper. Susan Levine, a reporter, phoned us to get more information. After a brief conversation she asked if she could visit us at our home. We double-checked with Alex. He still said, "Yes."

Susan Levine came over and sat with us in our living room for a few hours. A thin woman with short hair and round glasses, she has a bright-eyed look that makes you feel that everything you say is interesting. She was checking us out to see if we had a story. We were checking her out to see if she was someone that we felt we could trust. We chatted on about Alex and were soon laughing. Nanette started ruminating about the future and became teary-eyed. We told Susan how great the children at Alex's school had been to him, and Nanette cried.

Susan wanted to meet Alex. We called him up from the playroom. He came bounding up the stairs with his dry erase board and marker.

"Hi, Alex. Nice to meet you. I heard you saw a movie today."

Alex was tentative. He was looking down. The enthusiasm he had coming up the stairs was gone in a flash.

"What movie was it? Wait! Let me read your mind. Was it...*Star Wars*?"

Alex covered his ears and bent down. "Yes, how did you know?"

"I have magic powers."

Alex dropped to the floor and rolled halfway under the coffee table. I was starting to think this was a bad idea. Susan was trying to be ingratiating. She actually had a very pleasant manner, but her strategy was definitely not autistic. It probably would have worked on Simon, but not Alex.

Susan changed tactics. "I hear you like math. You got a perfect score on some big test."

Alex sprang to life. He grabbed his big, white dry erase board – almost as big as he was – and a marker.

"Can I ask you a math question?"

He poked his face into hers with a big smile, consciously trying to make eye contact. His face was smudged, as usual. His T-shirt was half hanging out of his cut-off shorts. His too long bangs were down to his eyebrows, but his countenance was bright and alive with an almost mischievous smile. Soon he was rambling on at warp speed talking about game theory and probability, tripping over his words, stopping and restarting his sentences, scrawling things on his board and erasing them with the palm of his hand which was quickly getting coated with blue ink.

In a five minute span, Susan saw him both withdrawing into his shell and embracing the world as best he could.

"Your son is so cute and charming. I hope I didn't upset him at first."

"It's just that he doesn't respond to social situations like most children."

Alex was back in the playroom. We talked for almost another hour.

"Well, I'd love to do a story if you'll let me."

We told her we'd call her. Both Nanette and I were impressed. She seemed very perceptive, and she seemed to genuinely like Alex. Since this would be a human interest story and not an investigative piece we felt secure that neither we nor anybody at Candlewood or in the neighborhood would be offended or taken to task. We told her we'd do it.

Susan came by again. And again. She visited Alex at school. Carol Guzman, a nationally known and award-winning photographer came as well. They followed Alex around school and hung out at our house. Carol, a friendly, athletic-looking woman with long blonde hair swept back in a ponytail, snapped roll after roll. She took hundreds of pictures. Alex played along at first, and actually had fun. After awhile, however, he started to get annoyed. We wondered why this was lasting so long.

Carol snapped him washing his face, swinging on the swing, jumping on the trampoline, staring out into space, and rolling on the floor. Once during the middle of all this she was paged by the paper. Annoyed, she told us she had to cover an event downtown with Muhammad Ali. She'd rather take pictures of Alex.

"What?" I thought. "You'd rather be in a suburban backyard with Alex than taking pictures of Muhammad Ali?"

Months later a friend told me to log onto the *Washington Post* website. "There are pictures of Alex there!"

Carol had won another major national award. She was cited for three photographic series: one for Mother Theresa's funeral, one for Muhammad Ali, and one for an autistic boy named Alex. I never thought I'd see those three names in the same sentence. Mother Theresa, Muhammad Ali, and Alex Mont.

The photographs of Alex were very moving. One showed him from behind as he stood in dim light looking out through our front door into the sunshine. Another had him lying down on the floor, smiling, but with his hand up blocking the camera. There was a picture of him crying under the table, holding his head, as his teacher comforted him. My favorite, though, was a close-up of him beaming, trying to look into the eyes of another little boy at school. He was obviously contemplating some private joke. Probably about math.

Finally, Susan and Carol were finished. Another day and we probably would have asked them to wrap it up. They were very pleasant, but we hardly felt we merited that much attention.

The story was set to be published in a few weeks, after school was finished for the year. We would be out of the country. My sister Debbie's oldest daughter, Rebecca, was having her Bat Mitzvah. They lived outside London, so we were going to make a vacation out of it. First England, and then Paris.

The trip was a blast. Simon loved the castles and the history and the knights in shining armor. Alex giggled constantly over the exchange rate, always letting us know the best places to convert our dollars into pounds or francs. The highlights of the trip for Simon were the Tower of London, touring the Roman baths, and going on a late night ghost walk. Alex particularly enjoyed learning the rules to cricket and the London Underground system. One of his favorite spots was visiting the Prime Meridian in Greenwich. Simon sampled Indian food in London and Moroccan food in Paris. With Alex we quickly learned how to say "pain" and "fromage" – French for bread and cheese. And to ask for our pasta "au natural", meaning with no sauce. Luckily, the world is a varied enough place to entrance both our sons, no matter their difference.

The last Sunday we were in Europe was the day the story on Alex was to be published. We were staying in a modern hotel in Paris – one with an internet connection. We logged on to the *Washington Post* webpage but couldn't find the story. Maybe they decided not to run it.

The next day we packed our things and grabbed a taxi to the airport. When we arrived home there were several papers on our porch, all of which were copies of Monday's *Washington Post*, all of which had a huge picture of Alex on the front page, above the fold. That morning he had been staring out, smiling from every news-stand in the metropolitan area.

When we arrived home, our message machine was full. Letters followed. Most of them were from parents of children with problems. One man was almost crying on the phone. They were all very thankful for sharing our story. Their gratitude made us feel we did the right thing.

We had some unexpected calls, too. One came from a man offering to teach Alex chess. We skipped that one. The expectation and pressure to be the next Bobby Fisher was something that Alex could live without.

The story was very long, practically an entire page. Susan did a wonderful job capturing Alex – his strengths and weaknesses. Five photographs accompanied the story. Our only complaint was the omission of Simon. We stressed during the interview what a great brother he was, but he was basically absent from the story. We told Simon that was a big, big mistake.

Alex was a celebrity. School was over or he might have been overwhelmed. People in the neighborhood and the kids at the community pool ran up to him very excited. A couple of the children mentioned in the story were quite pleased with their fame. The first couple of times people congratulated him he was happy. By the second day, however, he was annoyed.

"I KNOW I'm in the paper. Why are you telling me?"

He didn't like the attention. He also didn't understand why this was such a big deal. A producer at "Sixty Minutes" called us. Other television shows – the local news, "That's Incredible," "48 Hours" – followed. Alex was not interested. He didn't want the publicity, and we agreed. He was getting tired of people congratulating him for being in the newspaper. It was over and done with as far as he was concerned. Perhaps the scariest thing about television, though, was that the story would be out of our control. We said, "No."

The *Post* article was picked up by the military press and distributed overseas. We heard from someone in Korea. Regional papers reprinted the story. Old friends from graduate school were shocked to find Nanette and I in their local papers. After a couple of months, though, the story faded.

When I decided to write this book I sat down and talked with Alex. I told him I was going to write this book for me and for the family. I said other people might want to read it, too. That it might be helpful to moms and dads who had children like him. Would it be OK if I published it? He said, "Yes."

42

Life

❦

My mother was dying and my sons were growing up. Life ends. We work hard and struggle and love each other and then it's over. These are not novel thoughts. They are clichés. But they are also fundamental and terrifying truths.

I've always been afraid of death. Even phobic. The thought of non-existence terrifies me. To be no more? I took a class in Eastern religions in college. I learned that Buddhists think the idea of a conscious self is an illusion that must be overcome. I attended synagogue and saw true believers. I watched Christian Fundamentalists on TV news shows and marveled at their certainty. I wanted to believe in a higher meaning but I found I could not. Everything in my mind told me that all we have in life is this life. I started seriously evaluating my life. What I found mostly pleased me, but not entirely.

Alex and Simon were growing up. Simon was a good kid and he was happy. Alex, too, was happier. Remarkably, and with us barely realizing it at first, the boys started playing with each other some without too much intervention on our part. They were beginning to become a little self-sufficient – or at least a little better able to occupy themselves.

Nanette and I had more time for each other now. We actually had conversations in places other than bed. As fully as we loved and enjoyed our children, a post-child life was slowly coming into view and I found part of myself looking forward to it. Maybe that was because for the first time we could visualize an independent life for Alex. He had come such a long way already. We were starting to think the upper limit was higher than what we originally allowed ourselves to believe. Nanette and I even began to think of moving to the city when Simon went off to college.

"Then we can just walk to the movies or to the theater," said Nanette. "We'll be in the middle of everything."

"Yeah, we can do whatever we want to do." And when my kids are grown and out of the house, I thought, I'll have plenty of time to write and act and do the things I've longed for.

My mother was dying. I was having my first fantasies of retirement. Was I that tired? Or was I being like my mother?

"I love you, Daniel," she said, "and I love Debbie and Diane but I miss my little people. I knew the children but I don't really know the adults."

She had finally reached what was to be "her time." Unfortunately, it was spent going to doctors and tracking her deterioration.

"Mommy," I said at age eight. I had come to my parents' room in the middle of the night. I stood in the doorway in my pajamas. My mother turned over and looked up at me.

"What, Daniel? It's late."

"I'm afraid of dying."

"Daniel," she said, her voice growing softer. "You're only eight. I'm past thirty and I don't think about dying. You have years and years to live."

"But so what? So what if I live to a hundred? Still the day comes when you're dead and that's it. Forever."

"Honey, go back to bed and think of all the good things and fun things you've got to do in life. You're too young to think about death."

I looked at Simon who was then eight years old. It seemed like yesterday that I had that conversation with my mother. Maybe I really was approaching middle age. Isn't that when you start ruminating about how fast time passes?

I found myself thinking about my life and getting greedy. I was incredibly lucky. Nanette and I were still completely in love and remarkably almost on the same page in everything. My boys were healthy. My job was good. But I needed another passion. I needed to know that when "my time" came I had addressed every part of me. I feared regrets. I didn't want my next major life event to be retirement. I wanted part of "my time" now.

I went to my closet, pulled down a big box of old papers, and rifled through some old short stories and poems I had written years before. At one point, I had actually considered leaving graduate school to search for some other career. I took a semester off and attended a writing seminar taught by Lorrie Moore – then an up-and-coming author. Maybe, I thought, I should write again. I had toyed with the idea of writing a book about Alex. I had even scribbled down a few isolated memories from time to time.

I needed a release. I needed a release from all I was thinking. My mind also drifted back to my acting days and what a wonderful release that was.

"Nanette, would it be OK if I took an acting class? I need...I just don't want to wait to start doing something again."

"Sure, go ahead. You always talk about it. The kids are getting older. Go ahead. I'd like to finally see you on stage."

I dove into my acting class. Some part of me was liberated. Soon after that, I got my first small role in a community theater play. It had been almost 15 years since I had been on stage but I felt like a kid.

My parents came to see me in "The Skin of Our Teeth." They sat in the front row but my mother couldn't follow the play very well because it was a blur. Simon came up to me afterward and gave me a huge hug. In his eyes, I had been on Broadway. I had often seen his love for me in his face. This was the first time I saw pride. Soon he'd realize exactly where I was performing, but for the moment I just soaked it in and gave him a tour of backstage.

43

Math Camp

⍟

I know my time answering Alex's questions is limited. I have a PhD in economics and I taught econometrics in college. I have a minor in math from a top liberal arts college. I'm hoping these things can keep me one step ahead of Alex until he is at least in high school. The day he no longer thinks he can come to me with questions is going to be a very sad one for me. A big chunk of the time we connect and enjoy will be lost.

Our tutorial sessions became less frequent as Alex approached fourth grade. Sadly they have become more and more infrequent. By age ten, Alex was learning new math and science primarily from books. I bought a book on Fourier series for us to work through together. Fourier Series are sums of trigonometric functions used to represent periodic waves. After several chapters it became clear that he did not need me, so I left him to read on his own.

Already Alex figures out things that would escape me. During fifth grade he came home from school one day to report a tricky question on a test. Nanette was surprised that a school test could be tricky for Alex.

"You see, the question was this: you have two water bottles, each with the same volume of a different liquid. The liquids have different darknesses. If you lower a ball in one liquid it disappears at a depth of 3 centimeters. If you lower the ball in the other liquid it disappears at a depth of 8 centimeters. When would it disappear if you mixed the two liquids together?"

"I don't know," said Nanette, "How about at the mean, 5.5 centimeters?"

Alex cracked up. "You fell for the trick."

"What trick?"

"I thought it was the mean at first, but then I thought it couldn't be. Say you had two water bottles that were 60 centimeters high. Say the solution in one bottle was so close to clear that the ball didn't disappear until 59 centimeters, but it disappeared after 3 centimeters in the other bottle. Well, if you mixed the solutions and used the mean you'd get 31 centimeters but that couldn't be the right answer."

"Why?"

Alex is laughing so hard now he can barely get his sentences out. When he talks about things like this, he stops and restarts his sentences, laughs, and trips over his words because he can't get them out fast enough.

"Because basically you are mixing a clear solution with a dark one, and the mixture will be about half as dark as the original dark mixture. So if the ball disappeared at 3 centimeters in the first dark solution it will disappear at 6 centimeters in the solution that is half as dark. To account for this I used the harmonic mean, not the regular mean."

The harmonic mean is the reciprocal of the average of the reciprocals. The harmonic mean of 3 and 8 is $1/((1/3+1/8)/2)$, or about 4.44. When Alex checked his prediction experimentally, he was correct within one millimeter.

But Alex does not realize the extent of his abilities. He thought this was a trick designed by the test writer. He had no clue that there are very few fifth grade teachers in the country who even have any idea of what a harmonic mean is, let alone the ability to apply it to a new situation based on an intuitive grasp of what is going on in an experiment.

Alex has already won a number of math awards. He received a perfect score in the National Math Olympiad for fourth through sixth graders when he was in fourth grade. Over 85,000 students took the test, and only seven fourth graders got perfect scores. In fifth grade, he finished tied with two other children for second place in a national math talent search conducted by Johns Hopkins University. Almost 9000 students took this test, and in order to participate you had to have previously qualified by placing above the 97th percentile on a different standardized test.

When Alex's math prowess is confirmed by events such as these we are immensely proud. But more than that we are relieved. We hope that his math ability will buy him acceptance into the community and colleagues he can relate to. We fear his math ability may be the only thing that will allow him to be the eccentric and endearing math professor down the hall, and not the oddball at the end of the street.

Sometimes I take living with a mathematical marvel for granted. I must stop and remind myself that this elementary school student not only knows college level concepts but can out-think very intelligent adults.

Alex continually poses questions to himself – "How long will it take a basketball to hit the ground if dropped from ten feet" – and then answers them. He does this without complex math but with crystal clear reasoning. The basketball question is straightforward if you know calculus, but he didn't at the time. He basically intuited the calculus he needed in order to solve the problem.

We were walking down a grocery store aisle – still a favorite place – and Alex asked me what the formula for the area of an ellipse is.

"I don't know, Alex. We'll look it up when we get home."

"Can't you figure it out?" he smiled, a challenge in his voice.

"Alex, I would need to use calculus, I would have to have the equation of an ellipse and then integrate over it to get a formula for the area."

"I figured out a way without using complicated math."

Sure enough, he did. Using the relationship between the area of a circle and a square with sides equal to the diameter of that circle, he then thought about what happens as the square and the circle are stretched into a rectangle and an ellipse. He then derived the formula using fifth grade level arithmetic.

I could not have figured that out. I scored in the 99th percentile in every standardized math test I ever took when I was in school, minored in math, developed a mathematical model for my dissertation, and know a lot more higher level math than Alex. However, the ability to conceptualize a problem and think through it that Alex has, leaves me in the dust.

I sent the ellipse challenge to several of my friends. One is the director of a neurology training program with an MD from Harvard, another is a professor of public policy at Cornell University with a PhD in economics from Penn, and the third is a very creative middle school math teacher with a Masters in Education from Harvard. None of them came close to the answer.

Alex challenges me with math problems now more often than he comes to me for explanations. I dread the day he no longer thinks I'm worth the time.

Nanette is closer to dealing with this problem, and it saddens her. She fears the distance it might place between her and Alex. Nanette is no slouch when it comes to math. She took calculus in college and for awhile she considered becoming a math teacher when Alex was younger. In fact, it was Alex's infectious enthusiasm, creativity, and playfulness when it comes to math that inspired Nanette into thinking she could transfer that to other children. She went back to school when Simon entered pre-school and took classes in real analysis, geometry, and topology. When you stack her up against most people, she has an excellent facility for math. Alex, though, is not "most people," and their exchanges have become rare. He will occasionally ask her a question not to learn something but to see if she can figure it out. He'll look at me and say, "Daddy, don't give her the answer." That cuts her to the quick (of course sometimes I don't *know* the answer). I tell her not to worry, my day is coming, too.

Lately, though, Alex's ability to converse and connect seems to be broadening. As we fade away from his math life, hopefully there will be more opportunities to relate to him in other domains. And as Alex gets older, hopefully he will find more kindred spirits.

One place we thought he might find such like souls was at the Johns Hopkins University summer program for talented youth. We signed Alex up for an individually paced math curriculum course. We called it "math camp." It was a way to break up the long, monotonous summer, give Alex something he enjoyed, and hopefully let him interact with other precocious children who loved math.

Most of the children in that program were planning on completing coursework that would enable them to skip ahead to higher level classes in school. That wasn't our goal for Alex. We made it clear to his teacher that we wanted the summer to be fun and challenging. As far as we were concerned, Alex could work on any hodgepodge of math topics he desired.

Alex didn't do very well at the placement test that determined which class he'd be put in. He took the test in a room with the younger children, and although they weren't that noisy, the noise they did make bothered him a great deal. He was also upset at the wording of some of the questions. He ended up crying and was taken into another room so he could concentrate better on the test. By the time we picked him up, though, he was sad and agitated.

Things weren't much better at the first day of "camp," but then the program coordinator moved Alex up to the higher age group. The lower level of noise and the higher level of math activity worked like a charm. Alex ended up thoroughly enjoying the next three weeks.

His instructor, David, was a young doctoral student in math who was specializing in graph theory. David and Alex bonded quickly over their love of math. Sometimes Alex's exuberance posed a classroom management problem for David, but the summer went well.

One day when I was off from work, I went to pick up Alex a couple of hours early so I could observe what things were like at "camp." I arrived at 2:30. Class had started at 9:00. The kids had voted to eliminate their morning break so they could do more math, so by this time they had been working all day except for a half-hour break at lunch.

These children had been doing math at their desks all day. One boy was entering fourth grade; Alex was entering fifth, but most of the other children were in sixth through eighth grade. Each child was working at his or her own level and at his or her own pace. They were reading, solving math problems, and taking tests all day long. I walked into the classroom half expecting to see children ready to tear their hair out. But not one child was fidgeting. Not one child was daydreaming. All of them were busily working away, seemingly content. It was amazing.

At 3:00 it was time for the day's group activity. David put a famous problem up on the board – the Konigsburg bridge problem. This problem was the one that had inspired the famous mathematician Euler to develop the field of graph theory over a century earlier. There were a series of bridges in Kronigsburg and people often tried to figure out if it was possible to cross each bridge exactly once without having to retrace their steps. Proving that it was impossible led to the first major theorem in graph theory.

The kids giggled. They scribbled away. When David asked for comments, hands flew up and the children spewed forth very impressive insights. David asked if anyone could figure out the conditions for a graph being traceable in this way. Alex's hand shot up. He came to the board and probed Euler's theorem – which he had previously read about. He then went on to add some more facts and thoughts about graphs. It turned out that even in this class, Alex had developed a reputation as a math whiz.

The end of the day came and the children gathered their belongings and waited for their parents. Even after a long day of nothing but math, I saw graphing calculators being snatched out of backpacks as the children showed each other nifty things they had learned.

"In this group," I thought, "Alex could find friends."

The world is not that simple for Alex, though. On the last day of "camp" they had a math Jeopardy game and parents were invited. Nanette went. Because of the size of the class the children had to play in teams. Alex didn't like that. Other children would influence his score.

"What if they say the wrong answer but I know the right one? What if they talk while I'm trying to think?"

He couldn't take it. He quickly entered meltdown mode and Nanette rushed him from the room. She was distraught. If he couldn't fit in here, then where? She was practically in tears. She calmed Alex down, though, and got him to rejoin his team in time for the Final Jeopardy question.

"If you built a wall around the entire earth that was one foot high and walked around on top of it," said David, "How much further would you walk then if you walked directly alongside it?"

"Two pi feet!" Alex said in a loud whisper to his teammates.

"That can't be right."

"It's got to be way more than that."

"No! It's two pi feet!" said Alex getting louder and more anxious.

David quickly moved over towards Alex's team. "Did you say two pi feet?" Without pausing for an answer he said, "That's correct!"

Alex's team won. Alex was all smiles, the watery redness still not totally gone from his eyes. Everyone was impressed, but Nanette would have been much happier if he could only have managed to play the game. Even among the math whizzes, Alex stood apart.

44

Connections Gained and Lost

❦

Summer ended, and in the fall of 1997, just before Alex's tenth birthday, he entered fifth grade. That year would be his final year at Candlewood. He had been with his classmates for three years but he barely knew most of them. There were some signs, though, that he was beginning to make connections.

"Hey, Dan!" said Nanette, "I was at Marie's house today and you won't believe this. I was talking to Marie in the kitchen and Alex was playing some computer game with Kevin." Alex had been in class with Marie's son, Kevin, for over three years. He had been in cub scouts with him for two years. "Kevin came running into the room all excited. 'Guess what, Mom,' he shouted. 'Alex called me by my name!' He was thrilled. I don't know what bowled me over more, that Alex called him by name or that Kevin wasn't offended that it took three years."

There was a time I could go into Alex's kindergarten class and hang out for half an hour without him realizing that I was in the room. Now, he notices me at about the speed of a typical child. There was a time Alex would ask me to point out which child in a group was Simon. Now he can spot Simon at a distance. We're making progress.

In fourth grade, Alex had made his first friend. Johnny sat next to Alex in class. He had taught him jokes and high-five games. You can't imagine two such different boys. Alex is this small, out-of-it, bookish boy and Johnny is a big, strong kid with a buzz cut. He would actually be Alex's bodyguard on the playground. He once pushed a kid down who made fun of Alex. Not that I'd encourage that sort of thing, but part of me was glad. Nanette thought it was kind of sweet.

"Johnny has a really good heart," said Amy Cavanaugh, Alex's fourth grade teacher. "And he likes looking after Alex. He runs up to him to teach him some new high-five thing, like 'slap me high, slap me low...' and then pulling his hand away says, 'too slow!' They laugh and laugh."

"But the one he connected with the most," said Nanette, "is Kalita. She's the only child he refers to by name."

Kalita is a tall, African-American girl who towers over Alex. Like Johnny, she looked out for Alex. She was almost like a surrogate mom. Johnny and Kalita were the only children that Alex consistently recognized. They're the only kids that elicited smiles. They cared for him and were at ease with him. He sensed that. Most people in the world move about Alex in a whirl. The fact that he could pick these two out makes us hopeful he can have friends in the future.

Often you have to try to find humor in situations. By fifth grade, Alex was able to compete on a county recreational basketball team. We received special permission for Alex to play on Simon's third grade team. His skill level was still among the lowest and being small he was shorter then almost half of the other children. It was a major step that he could play without getting upset about "fairness." In fact, he loved the organizational trappings – the time clock, the scoreboard, the numbers on the uniform – he even loved whenever the referee would signal for any type of infraction. But watching Alex guard a child during a game is hysterical. Since he cannot recognize faces he has to keep going around people to see the number on their backs. Unfortunately, this creates lay-up opportunities for the other team and some pretty bizarre scenes as Alex quickly darts behind the opposing player as he is passed the ball to see if he should be guarding him. He is very intense and determined but not very effective. I breathe a sigh of relief if a child is wearing shorts of a unique color or has some glaring characteristic – maybe he has red hair or is the only child of a particular race. Alex can guard that player and his defense improves tremendously. In fact, he is so intense at his task he can sometimes drive his opponent nuts, guarding him closely even when the ball is on the opposite end of the court or even out of play.

One relationship that was very special to Alex and to me was the one he had with my mother. He had a wonderful bond with my mother from a very early age, even when his ability to connect with most people was close to non-existent. She would get right down on the floor with him and play games. More than that, she simply accepted him for who he was. She was a large woman, and would wrap him up in her arms, and he'd let her.

Alex has no social graces. He says things exactly as they are.

"Hi, Alex. Come up here and let me hug you."

"Hi Grandma! Why are you so fat?"

"Because I eat too much. Why are you so cute?"

Many people feel awkward or uncomfortable around Alex, not sure how to act. My mom never freaked out or felt uncomfortable around him. Alex would touch her face and ask her math questions. She couldn't answer them, and Alex would laugh. She'd laugh, too.

My mom's condition deteriorated. She came to school to see Alex get an award but she could no longer see his face. The walk from the car to the school left her winded. She was in constant pain. Even Simon noticed, but she laughed him off when he mentioned it.

The entire time I was growing up, I can almost never recall hearing my mother complain about her health or anything in her life. She might complain about how messy me and my sisters were, or about her boss at work, but even during my father's illnesses or during bouts of complications she had related to her diabetes she never complained.

Around this time, though, she began to open up to me, and that's when I knew things were serious. She was in a panic over the fact that she was going blind. She thought life would not be worth living. As her condition deteriorated, walking from the living room to the kitchen was something she had to brace herself for.

"I'm scared, Daniel. I feel like I'm dying. I'm not ready to die. I'm only 60. Damn it! This was supposed to be my time. Now I can't even walk or go to a movie. I was going to travel." She started crying. I didn't know what to say. I tried to give her hope. I felt inadequate. I felt less than inadequate; I felt worthless. It was obvious to all of us that my mother's condition was not going to improve. There wasn't any realistic hope, but how could I admit that to her? I tried to amuse her with stories of Simon and Alex. There was that gap between the dying and the not yet dying that I couldn't breech.

My father stood by her side and nursed her. He was devoted to her, but he sometimes needed to get out himself. One night he went out and I sat with her for a couple of hours. She slept the whole time, fading in and out. She sat inches away from a large TV screen as her VCR played *Showboat*. She loved old musicals, but she ignored the screen. We talked a little. I noticed that she showed little fear or anger over her condition, that night. She seemed resigned to it. My Dad returned and I went home.

Later that night, the phone rang and woke me up. I ran to the kitchen.

"Who's calling at this hour?" mumbled Nanette.

"It's bad news. I know it."

I fumbled with the light and answered the phone. It was my father. He sounded strained and strangely formal.

"Dan, it's Dad. I was calling because I thought I should let you know."

He was trying to sound calm.

"What's wrong?"

"The ambulance is here. They're trying to revive Mom." His voice broke. "I just thought I should tell you."

"I'm on my way."

I threw some clothes on.

"Nanette, I'm going over to my parents'. The paramedics are there. They are trying to revive my mother."

"Oh my God!"

"I know."

I flew out the door and jumped in the car. The trip was six miles but it felt like sixty. I tried hard to concentrate on the road. When I pulled into the parking lot at the townhouse complex, I saw my father strapping his seatbelt on in the front seat of the ambulance. His door was still open so the light was on. He was terrified. He pulled the door shut as the ambulance drove away.

I parked the car and ran over to some firefighters who were loading equipment into their truck. Their faces told me all I needed to know, but I refused to believe it.

"That woman is my mother. Is she OK?"

"We aren't allowed to say anything."

"Which hospital are they taking her to?"

"Montgomery General."

I ran back to my car and drove to the hospital. I must have driven fast because when I got there they were taking my mother out of the back of the ambulance and into the emergency room. She was dressed in a nightgown, lying flat on her back. She had a portable respirator attached to her that made her chest heave up and down unnaturally. One of her arms hung loosely at her side. I saw them usher my father in through a different door. I parked the car and went inside. My dad was in the waiting room, trembling. He was the only one there. He kept telling me that this couldn't be happening, that she'd be all right. There was a hole burning in my stomach. He asked me to call Debbie and Diane.

I went over to the payphone and called Debbie. As soon as I started speaking with her the receptionist came up to me.

"Hold on a second, Debbie." I turned to the receptionist.

"Mr Mont," she said. "They're calling for the chaplain."

I broke down but tried to talk through my sobbing.

"They just told me they're calling for the chaplain."

I knew from the look in the receptionist's eyes that my mother was dead but I couldn't bring myself to say those words to Debbie. I thought she'd understood. She still thought there was time to see my mother alive one last time, though, and loaded up her family and started driving down from New Jersey. Later that night – actually early in the morning – I called Diane and told her. She screamed. I told her to come to my house.

When I told Simon he burst into sobs and hugged me with all his strength. He sat around with the family and looked at old photographs and cried and laughed. Alex showed almost no emotion, but I could hear the gears grinding in his head.

"Alex, do you want to go to Grandma's funeral?"

"YES." His eyes were downcast but his voice was emphatic.

We drove up to New Jersey, and buried my mom on a cold, gray day in December. Our family's section of the cemetery had too many tombstones of relatives who had died in their fifties and sixties, often from conditions linked to diabetes. The rabbi read a speech that Debbie, Diane, and I had written. My dad managed to say a few words. The weight of our loss was heavy. Afterwards, we walked across the damp cemetery to our cars and drove back to Debbie's house to sit shiva. Alex was quiet and attentive. He didn't say anything. I kept thinking of all the things my mom never got to do. And that I couldn't believe she was gone, that I could never call her up to tell her the latest little thing one of my boys did. And how at the end of my life, I didn't want to have a list of things I never got around to doing. I resolved to do the things I always wanted to do – to write, to act, to balance my life. I also resolved never to let Alex and Simon forget my mom. They were so young. She could easily become a distant memory.

Back at Debbie's house I would glance at Alex. When I brought the subject of my mother up he waved me off almost in panic.

That evening, members from Debbie's synagogue came over to her house to say Kaddish, the Jewish prayer for mourning. We gathered in the living room and passed out prayer books. Alex and Simon stood next to me, with yarmulkes that were too big for their heads. We started praying. We rarely go to services but Simon goes to Hebrew school and Alex has a tutor so they could basically say the prayer with us. Alex held his book in front of him and intently followed along, trying to read the words. By the end of the prayer his eyes were heavy with tears. He wiped them away, closed the book, and stood silently, his face red.

"Alex, do you miss Grandma?"

"Yes."

"Me, too."

When we got back home I could only sleep in fits and starts. I dreamed about my mother and I would wake up with the sound of her voice in my ears. How long before that faded? And I thought about death. I tried not to, but I was drawn to it like a moth to a flame. My mom's death. My death. I tried to hide my fear from Nanette, but I constantly fell to thinking about it.

My mother had always said that her life was a success because my life was a success. What is a success?

"I'm going to write that book, Nanette. The book about Alex. I've been talking about it for years, and I'm going to do it."

It would be gift to both my mother and my sons. I wanted to show my mom that her life and death moved me to embrace all of my life. To follow a passion.

I wrote the first draft of the book on the 45-minute train ride to and from work, and sometimes over lunch. It poured out of me. When time came for serious rewriting Nanette let me work four days a week instead of five to solidify it. She was also my fact checker.

"That's not what happened, Dan. You've got the order screwed up."

She was usually right. Sometimes, though, she would become annoyed or almost offended.

"You seem upset," I said. "What's wrong?"

"You're leaving out some really important parts. Stuff I went through. You say 'her day was tough' but there was so much more there."

"But I wasn't there. I mean, I'm writing from my memories. I was at work much of the time you were with the kids. I think I've put a lot about what you went through."

"I just have to get used to the fact that you are writing OUR story from YOUR point of view. It's really your book."

"It's the only way I can write it."

It's tough and even uncomfortable looking at your life that closely. Writing has made me more aware of things and more aware of who's narrating. But I'm more aware of life now and the limited time I have. And I want all our lives to be filled to the brim.

45

Graduation

∽

Fifth grade was nearing its end, and the ugly specter of middle school loomed in front of us. Fifth grade had been a relatively good year. Alex's teacher, Mike, a lanky, balding, and bespectacled man in his fifties, got along with Alex very well. Mike can get exasperated easily, and Alex's inability to stay in his seat, his unceasing questioning, and his lack of proper classroom decorum can exasperate the best of them. But he did a great job integrating him with the rest of the class as best he could and did a marvelous job at getting Alex to write, something he has always had great difficulty with. His writing assignments were creative and manageable and his feedback was copious.

Some parents have a difficult time with Mike because of his sarcastic sense of humor and his in-your-face attitude, but most children love him. Often I would see former students coming to visit him after school hours. The reason, I believe, is that he talks and deals with his students more like they are little adults and not children. At that pre-adolescent age, I think they appreciate that level of respect.

"I would love to teach Alex one-on-one. He is an amazing student. He loves learning and he is brilliant. But as part of a class...I just don't see how he can manage in a regular middle school setting. The main thing that has made this year successful," said Mike, "was how accepting the other children are."

"What do you mean?" I asked.

"Well, take for example the spelling bee. Alex won the class spelling bee, but he was laughing every time someone spelled a word incorrectly."

"Oh, God, that's terrible."

"I know. I tried to get him to stop but the other children didn't seem to mind. If anybody else had done that it would have been really hurtful."

"Alex was just laughing at something being incorrect. He wasn't really making fun of the other kids…"

"I know that. But what amazes me is that the children know that. When he won the spelling bee they actually all gave him a big round of applause. They were all rooting for him. They always seem to be rooting for him."

"That's amazing."

"Especially when he shows me up. The other day during math class, Alex once again corrected me. I put up a list of rules for knowing if a number is divisible by another number."

"You mean like you know any number ending in five or zero is divisible by five and that a number, like 2313, is divisible by three because the digits of that number add up to a number that is also divisible by three?"

"Right. But I said there was no simple rule for knowing if something was divisible by seven. Alex started laughing. I said, 'OK, Alex go to the board and show me.' Sure enough, he knew a way."

"Yeah, he's a never-ending source of little tidbits like that."

"But he has big problems working with groups in any kind of cooperative way. He doesn't know when it is OK to speak and when he should be quiet. He is incapable of organizing his belongings, and he gets very upset at small things. Sometimes he even throws himself at the floor. And he doesn't know who anybody is. He came up to me just the other day and referring to his classmates said, 'Who are these people and why are they making so much noise?'"

"I know. I know."

"Without Kalita, sometimes I don't know how I'd manage. At times she's almost like an aide."

As fifth grade neared its end, we knew we'd have to leave the Candlewood community behind. Alex couldn't deal with a regular program at a regular middle school. After much searching – and many rejections from private schools – we decided upon a gifted and talented learning disabled program in a public school. The classes were small, the teachers had experience with special needs children, and, truth be told, it was our only option. What was heartening, though, was the genuine enthusiasm they had at the thought of having Alex.

On graduation day, Nanette, Simon, my Dad and I filed into the all-purpose room. All the other families took their seats. The room was packed. Blue and gold decorations lined the walls. The graduating class met elsewhere in the building and then marched in and took their assigned places. The children looked all grown up and like little babies both at the same time. I tried to imagine what their faces would be like when they were adults.

They sang songs. Alex just mouthed the words, but he stood with the other children patiently. John, the first boy who looked out for him in second grade, and Emily, the little girl who had thought he was so "modern" for not picking on girls, gave speeches. The principal wished them a fond farewell. Flowers and diplomas were passed out and the parents snapped photographs and clapped. Afterwards there were sodas and home-baked goods.

"So Alex, congratulations. You're a fifth grade graduate! Next stop, middle school!"

"Can we go home now?"

Alex's classmates were scurrying around signing each other's autograph books. A bunch of kids ran up to Alex asking for his signature. He obliged but he wasn't interested in getting their signatures. After a short while we headed out the door. A remembrance authored by each of the graduating students was printed in the autograph books. I took Alex's book and thumbed through it, looking for his:

> In third grade my class did current events. This meant that students had to write a short report putting a recent news article in their own words. There were two groups. Each week a group would read their current events. The next week the other

group would do it. It would keep alternating like this so that each group performed once every two weeks. My teacher gave two percentage grades for each report, one for written expression and one for oral expression. The maximum grade was 95 per cent. Why? The answer is: nobody is perfect.

46

Becoming Self-Aware

❦

Alex is becoming more self-aware and that thrills and terrifies me.
He is beginning to more fully understand that he is different from
other people. Being self-aware is a sign that he comprehends the world
around him better. He'll need to do that in order to successfully adapt to
it. On the other hand, it may be a sign that there is pain in his future.

"Alex, you are making a mess. Could you try to be neater? That
icecream is getting all over the place."

"OK! How neat should I be?"

I know what's coming. His voice starts getting more high-strung.

"Alex," says Simon, "Just don't drip it all over the place."

"OK. Minimum drip allowance is 4.36 micrograms. Minimum
eating speed is 4567 molecules per minute." His voice grows louder and
more agitated with each number.

"Oh, come on, Alex. What's the big deal? You can eat the ice cream,
but if you start seeing drips all over the table it is a sign you are being too
messy. Eat over the table. Don't take too much in your spoon. Just try to
be neat."

"OK, exactly what do you mean by 'neat'?"

I get exasperated and yell. Eventually, we calm down. I start talking
to him about other times when I say he is moving too slowly and he
starts running around like a maniac being as fast as he can.

"All I mean, Alex, is that I want you to move at a reasonable, normal speed because otherwise we'll be late."

"What do you mean, like four miles per hour?"

"Alex! Nobody thinks, 'I'll move at four miles per hour.' You just sort of gauge your speed from what is normally done in that kind of situation. I don't even know what it means to get dressed at four miles per hour."

"Well, how come everybody else seems to know how fast to go?"

I am taken aback.

"And how come everybody else know the rules for eating neatly? How can people be smart enough to learn all those rules? There are so many different situations."

"People don't really think about the rules explicitly, Alex. It's more like trial and error, adjusting yourself to the situation."

"But how do they know how to do it?"

"You only need a couple of rules. Rule number one: try not to make a mess. Rule number two: if you see that you are beginning to make a mess, figure out why and adjust."

My heart bleeds. What a daunting task.

I wrote into the autism website asking for help. I was told by an autistic adult that at Alex's age if someone told him to be neater such instructions would have been useless. They would have been worse then useless, they would have been infuriating. What do you mean by "neat"? Can't you define that more precisely? He sent me a list of about ten rules describing neat eating. Starting with things like – "for most foods, food should be kept on your plate, an eating utensil, or in your mouth." I showed the rules to Alex. He thought they were helpful but incomplete.

"Alex, you know you're not supposed to walk on the couch, especially with shoes on!"

"OK, rule number 6562! How am I supposed to keep all these rules in my head? Give me up to three rules maximum to remember at any one time."

"You don't need to be thinking about all the rules all the time!"

"Isn't that how other people do it?"

"No."

"Then how do they know? How can they be so smart?"

"Alex, you are autistic."

Adolescence is approaching. For a normal, well-adjusted child this is not an easy time. For a child like Alex? It's unfathomable. Luckily, Alex seems to be maturing slowly, but we're bracing for the storm. With Alex, it will be an adventure. It will be hard. It will be funny. And I'm going to learn more rules than I can possibly keep in my head.

Epilogue

On Veteran's Day, Alex's middle school had an open house. He is adjusting to school, but his main problems are in the hallways. I decided to shadow him down the hall. Alex is practically the shortest kid in the school. On that day he was wearing a math T-shirt and a huge backpack. He held the straps out away from his body with his thumbs like they were suspenders. His glasses were crooked and his shoelaces were untied. Half of his shirt stuck out. He could have had "nerd" stamped on his back.

Alex zipped down the hallway oblivious to the other kids. He wove in and out among them like they were an obstacle course. He cut off three tall boys in baggy pants. They were talking loud and confidently. One of them was taller than me. Alex cut them off so sharply they had to pull up short not to run him over.

"Do you see that kid?" said the tallest one.

"Yeah?"

"That kid is the..."

I was expecting...the most spaced out ...rudest ...nerdiest ...smartest ...oddest?

"That kid is the coolest kid in this school."

"What?" I thought.

"What?" said one of the other boys.

"No, he's right, man," said the last boy. "That kid is cool!"

"Why?"

"Man, the other day I saw some teacher telling him it was time to sit down and, bam, he sat down. Right in the hall."

"Yeah, that boy has got some serious sass."